Come to the Feast

Invitational Evangelism

Roberto Escamilla

DISCIPLESHIP RESOURCES

P.O. BOX 840 • NASHVILLE, TENNESSEE 37202-0840

www.discipleshipresources.org

Dedication

This book is dedicated to my gifted wife, Dorothy Mae,
our four wonderful children and their spouses, as well as
to the ten grandchildren who individually and collectively
make my life a constant celebration—a "fiesta!"

Cover and book design by Sharon Anderson

ISBN 0-88177-231-3

Library of Congress Catalog Card No. 98-86149

Scripture quotations, unless otherwise indicated, are from the New Revised Standard
Version of the Bible, copyright © 1989 by the Division of Christian Education of the
National Council of the Churches of Christ in the USA. All rights reserved. Used by
permission.

DR231

Contents

ACKNOWLEDGMENTS 4

PREFACE 6

INTRODUCTION 9

CHAPTER ONE:
Unexpected Invitation:
Toward a Theology for Evangelism 21

CHAPTER TWO:
Invitational Preaching in the Twenty-First Century:
Preaching for a Response 41

CHAPTER THREE:
Invitation to Healing and Wholeness:
The Unanswered Question of Suffering and Pain 63

A CONCLUDING WORD 79

Acknowledgments

I am deeply indebted to the Foundation for Evangelism; to its former president, Bishop Earl Hunt, Jr.; and to its current president, Bishop Ernest Fitzgerald. I am also indebted to the executive vice-president of the Foundation for Evangelism, Paul Ervin; to the chairperson of its board of directors, Roy Warren; as well as to the board of the Foundation for sponsoring the Denman Lectures in conjunction with our 1998 Congress on Evangelism: "Inviting a Changing World to the Changeless Christ." I also thank the Foundation for Evangelism for sponsoring the E. Stanley Jones Chair of Evangelism in a number of United Methodist-related seminaries in this country and overseas. I am very proud to be occupying the E. Stanley Jones Chair of Evangelism at Methodist Theological School in Ohio.

The Council on Evangelism and its president, Dr. Stewart Greene; the field consultant, Dr. Charles G. Whittle; as well as the whole Executive Committee of the Council deserve a special word of recognition.

I would like to express a word of loving memory and faithful recognition to our beloved Harry Denman, for whom these lectures are named. I met Brother Harry many years ago when I first joined the staff of the former Board of Evangelism in Nashville, Tennessee. It is highly appropriate that I have given these memorial lectures the general title of "Invitational Evangelism," for Brother Harry was always about the "invitation business."

I would like to express sincere thanks to the following people:

▲ Dr. Paul Escamilla, James Delaplain, David Escamilla, and Dr. Donald Mauck have all read the material and have made very creative suggestions.

▲ Sally Casto on the faculty of Methodist Theological School in Ohio was kind enough to read the manuscript.

▲ Sharon Douglas deserves special recognition for spending countless hours tirelessly typing and retyping the manuscript.

▲ Datha Myers, faculty secretary at Methodist School of Ohio, and Virginia Hildebrand helped in numerous ways.

▲ Alan Waltz, publisher of Discipleship Resources, and Hendrik Pieterse, my editor, showed patience and understanding throughout this process.

The list would not be complete without including special thanks to Dr. Jeffrey Hopper, who made significant contributions to the book, and to Dr. Ned Dewire and Dr. Robert Tannehill, the President and Dean of the Methodist Theological School in Ohio, respectively, for their kind encouragement and support.

It was E. Stanley Jones who first planted in my heart the desire to be an "evangelist," as he himself wanted to be known. To his memory I owe a special debt of gratitude, for I consider myself to be an evangelist regardless of what other titles I may have at the moment.

I am indebted for all of my thoughts to the authors whom I have quoted. In a very real sense I am also indebted to many others who, even though I have not quoted them, are very much a part of my own theological understanding, for they have impacted my life one way or another.

As I review the list of those who have preceded me in delivering the Denman Lectures, I can honestly say that each of them, without exception, has influenced my own life. I have heard almost every one of them personally for the last thirty-four years and then read their materials repeatedly. Just to mention a few, I would certainly list Albert C. Outler, Bishop Roy Nichols, Dr. Ellsworth Kalas, Bishop Emerson S. Colaw, and more recently Bishop Earl G. Hunt, who rang the bell loud and clear with his great lecture series on "Evangelism for a New Century." My thanks also go to Barbara Brokoff, who is a great evangelist and who preceded me in delivering the 1996 Denman Lectures.

And last but not the least, to my wife, Dorothy Mae: She has shared in depth the issues and concerns on the subject of evangelism with me for over forty-five years, has read the manuscript for this book and made many creative suggestions, and has sacrificially given of herself to enable many good things to happen.

Preface

Evangelism is back on the agenda of the church! For some years, evangelism was either ignored or placed in an obscure corner of the room. In other cases, it has gotten some "bad press," due partly to abuses that have taken place, particularly through the electronic church. But the 1996 General Conference stated clearly that the mission of The United Methodist Church is "to make disciples of Jesus Christ." That alone puts evangelism officially back on the agenda of the church.

Every time evangelism is given a narrow definition in terms of "saving souls" and nothing else, evangelism gets bad press. Naturally, saving souls is not the only thing the gospel is about: The gospel is an invitation to the whole person—soul and body—to come to Christ.

Furthermore, it is rather unfortunate that we allow the dichotomy between evangelism and social issues to take place. There is really no way to separate personal evangelism and issues of advocacy and social justice. It should never be a matter of either/or but always both/and; personal evangelism and social concern belong together.

I have always been fascinated with the concept of the gospel as an *invitation*. I believe that evangelism is an invitation that is extended to every person everywhere. I remember well my esteemed friend of many years, Charles D. Whittle, saying over and over again, "We must get back into the invitation business!" The "old-fashioned" idea of asking people to come to Christ must be recovered. People will come, but they need to be asked!

Think of a congregation with an average attendance in Sunday worship of, let's say, two hundred. Of these two hundred people, envision one hundred totally committed to extending to others the invitation to come to Christ. Let's imagine further that each of these hundred people meets at least five individuals in a given week and invites them to church. Of the five people, let's say (rather conservatively) at least two come on a given Sunday. With proper follow-up, it is conceivable that one of the two people would join the church. Well, you can do the math; the point is that you could literally add hundreds of new people to a congregation and thus reverse the serious membership loss that is taking place in United Methodism. Recall Acts 2:47:

"And day by day the Lord added to their number those who were being saved."

Of course, for all this to happen you need a truly evangelistic environment in the church. Such an environment should have at least the following characteristics:

▲ People's needs are met.

▲ There is a sense of the presence of God.

▲ There is a personal experience of the saving grace of Christ.

▲ Prayer is a reality and is practiced regularly.

▲ The Bible is preached with power as the word of God.

Indeed, we must get back into the "invitation business" in every possible way!

The title for these published lectures includes the term *feast* (*fiesta* in Spanish). I chose the term because I believe that the gospel is not only an invitation to come home but also a celebration for those who have come home. The gospel is celebration, and evangelism is celebration—a fiesta! "Let us eat and celebrate [fiesta]; for this son of mine was dead and is alive again; he was lost and is found!" (Luke 15:23-24). I believe that God does not want us to lead miserable lives.

Somehow we have forgotten how to celebrate. We are so intense in our theologizing that we don't have time to celebrate. When we talk about a seeking God, we have ample reason to celebrate. It is not just a theological concept. It is a reality. It is a celebration. It has to do with an inner life of faith.

In his "Hispanic Creed," Justo González included a significant phrase about the "Great Fiesta" that conveys the basic idea of celebration:

We believe in the Reign of God—the day of the Great Fiesta,
when all the colors of creation will form a harmonious rainbow,
when all peoples will join in joyful banquet,
when all tongues of the universe will sing the same song.[1]

The main part of *Come to the Feast* consists of an introduction and three chapters. The introduction sets the stage for the rest of the material. In it, I establish some basic theological understandings about the meaning of evangelism in order to put the discussion to follow in the proper context.

---

1 From "Hispanic Creed," by Justo González, in *Mil Voces Para Celebrar: Himnario Metodista*; © 1996 Abingdon Press; published by The United Methodist Publishing House; page 70. Used by permission.

In Chapter One, "Unexpected Invitation: Toward a Theology for Evangelism," I set forth the basic theological understandings of evangelism. In Chapter Two, "Invitational Preaching in the Twenty-First Century: Preaching for a Response," I discuss what I consider to be one of the most important aspects of evangelism today: preaching, or proclamation—that is, the "kerygma." In Chapter Three, "Invitation to Healing and Wholeness: The Unanswered Question of Suffering and Pain," I discuss the issue of healing and wholeness, not as an end in itself but as part of the journey toward maturity.

At the end of each chapter, there are some questions for reflection and discussion. These questions may be helpful, particularly if the book is used as a small-group study or for a Sunday school class.

Invitational theology holds that God accepts us in spite of our sinful condition—we are accepted by God. All we have to do is accept the fact that God has *already* accepted us. As Paul tells us, "While we still were sinners Christ died for us" (Romans 5:8).

As you read this book, pray for a new spiritual awakening, not only in this country but also around the world.

Introduction

To set things in their proper perspective and thus build an operational framework for these lectures, let me say a word about the cultural setting of the twenty-first century in which we must not only serve people but also overcome all the obstacles to the task of evangelization. I am not pleading for any kind of "faddish" theology, but I am talking about the need to have a clear understanding of what we are about as Christians, and at the same time have the ability to read the signs of the times (Matthew 16:3). It is necessary to interpret accurately our cultural situation.

What kind of definition of evangelism will be appropriate for this postmodern and secularized world? I make the basic assumption that the revelation of God in Jesus Christ addresses the crisis of any culture at any place and at any time in history. "Jesus Christ is the same yesterday and today and forever" (Hebrews 13:8). Therefore, the general theme for the 1998 Congress on Evangelism, "Inviting a Changing World to the Changeless Christ," is highly appropriate. I trust that we can disengage the gospel from many of the cultural trappings in which the gospel may find itself. Unfortunately, the church has quite often become a mirror of the culture that surrounds it. Therefore, we need to find a way to free the church and disengage it from that tendency. Furthermore, I am making the basic assumption that the United States of America is a mission field just as important as any other mission field in the world.

I believe that evangelization is a highly complex task and that we need an intelligent and honest approach to secular people. We cannot afford the luxury of being simplistic or of engaging in platitudes that turn people off. Rather, we must follow the example of Jesus, who was able to penetrate the inner life and consciousness of people. A good example is the Samaritan woman who came to get water from the well (John 4:1-42). Jesus first listened to her and answered her question; then he offered her a different kind of water that would spring up to everlasting life (John 4:14).

Now you and I know that no one really opposes evangelism; it would be like opposing motherhood. We all give either partial or total support to the idea of spreading the good news to others.

So, what's the problem? The problem is found, I think, at the local church level: Many congregations consider evangelism to be something peripheral to their main activities. At best, evangelism is tolerated; tragically, in many other congregations it is simply ignored. Some people say that everything the church does is evangelism. This statement has just enough truth in it to be misleading, or at least to be a source of confusion. It is true that everything the church does is—or ought to be—redemptive. However, the problem is that because of that assumption (which is sound theology), the specific task of evangelism does not always get done. It becomes everybody's responsibility, and thus nobody's responsibility.

Assigning the specific work of evangelism to a group of people (task force or committee) who will take on that responsibility and be held accountable for it is more practical than assuming that the whole church will be involved automatically in doing evangelism.

In a highly secularized society, people still come asking questions. They need the living water (John 4:10). A fairly contemporary song says, "People need the Lord!" Such a friendly confrontation with the gospel enables people to find purpose and meaning in their existence.

I recently attended a meeting of the Academy for Evangelism in Theological Education in Kansas City. The invited lecturer was the well-known author Lyle E. Schaller, who is considered to be one of the best-known sociologists of religion in America. He discussed primarily the content of his recent book, which has the rather intriguing and challenging title *Tattered Trust: Is There Hope for Your Denomination?* Schaller contends that all Protestant denominations, including The United Methodist Church, will experience difficult times in the future. One of the primary reasons he gives is that these denominations haven't developed strategies for mission and evangelism.[2]

On my way to the meeting, I flew over Memphis, Tennessee. We were flying on top of a heavily overcast sky. Above us were also heavy layers of dark clouds; however, on the far horizon was a strip of clear blue sky and the marvel of the rising sun. Even before hearing Schaller's lectures and in the midst of reading his book, I thought: *Yes, there are dark clouds beneath, and there are even darker clouds above, but there is hope for our denomination; it is symbolized in that bright, clear horizon and the rising sun.*

---

2 Discussed in *Tattered Trust: Is There Hope for Your Denomination?* by Lyle E. Schaller (Abingdon Press, 1996).

The question is, How are we in the church going to get a sense of compelling direction? If it is true that there is a leadership crisis in most institutions, including the church, the question is, How are we going to get the kind of leadership that will carry the gospel into the new millennium? We need to know how we are going to minister to the needs and the expectations of a new generation. We need to have a clear understanding of the nature of the crisis behind the stained glass, as someone has said. The question is, How are we going to interpret the nature of the crisis? At this point, we have many diagnosticians but very few, if any, authorities who would prescribe a solution.

Alan K. Waltz has made an outstanding contribution regarding the future of our denomination in his highly creative book, *To Proclaim the Faith*. In the book, he says: "Our challenge today is to continue as the people of the assurance, to affirm individuals in God's grace, and to reform and change where needed. If we do not proclaim, sustain, and serve with great assurance, then we fail."[3]

Schaller believes that many of our denominational systems unfortunately have become dysfunctional. The truth is that the new generations are no longer guided by the same criteria that guided their parents in selecting a church that, among other things, would have relevance to their spiritual journey. Among the critical issues that the postmodern generation rates as highly significant is the need to understand what it means to be a Christian, what is required in one's spiritual journey, and especially, what it means to accept Jesus Christ as Lord and Savior.

We are all alarmed by the serious and devastating membership losses that are taking place in almost every annual conference in The United Methodist Church.[4] Schaller, who understands deeply the sociological scenarios that prevail today, contends that physical death alone is enough to cause serious membership loss. Then he raises the important question: What are the most effective ways to reach younger generations and recent immigrants with the gospel of Jesus Christ? To answer this question, I believe we need a clear definition of evangelism. For the purpose of these lectures, let me state my working definition of evangelism:

---

3 From *To Proclaim the Faith*, by Alan K. Waltz; © 1983 the General Council on Ministries of The United Methodist Church; published by Abingdon Press; page 133.
4 For a statistical analysis, refer to *Tattered Trust: Is There Hope for Your Denomination?* by Lyle E. Schaller (Abingdon Press, 1996); pages 90–131.

> Evangelism is the dynamic witness of the love and grace of God as revealed in Jesus Christ and the invitation to all people to make a decision of accepting Christ as their personal Savior and Lord. This initial decision (conversion) is followed by a lifelong journey of growth, maturity, and service in the church as Christ's disciples.

Why would some people resist even a balanced definition of evangelism such as this one? I think it has to do with certain images that come to mind whenever the word *evangelism* is mentioned. Sometimes the image is of rural and small-town America; at other times the image is associated with patriotism and old-fashioned family values. At still other times, people associate evangelism with some kind of anti-intellectualism.

Many people still think of evangelism as somewhat related to prayer retreats for spiritual renewal, whose influence never goes beyond the threshold of the church door and which reflects total lack of concern for others. Many times we think of evangelism as what happens at national conferences or regional events (such as the Congress on Evangelism), where some type of training and inspiration takes place, but then we go home and do nothing. I could go on and on listing images and word associations. But the issue is to find out what evangelism really is or what evangelism needs to be as we enter the twenty-first century.

However, we need to go much further and deal with the realities of the so-called post-Christian world. In his book *The Crisis in the Churches: Spiritual Malaise, Fiscal Woe*, Robert Wuthnow affirms that there is a spiritual malaise in the life of the church that has silently grown during the past decade.[5]

There are many questions that seem to cry out for some kind of answer:

▲ How do we identify with a given community?
▲ How do we become the voice of the voiceless?
▲ How do we respond to the awesome problems of hunger for bread?
▲ How does a contemporary person meet Christ in a meaningful way?

---

5 Discussed in *The Crisis in the Churches: Spiritual Malaise, Fiscal Woe*, by Robert Wuthnow (Oxford University Press, 1997).

▲ How do we translate God's grace in the here and now?

▲ What does it mean to say that God loves us and forgives us?

There are no simple answers to these and many other questions. Ours is now a highly pluralistic society that requires multiple approaches to the task of communicating the gospel.

There are models that may help us experiment with possible answers in our quest to communicate the gospel with integrity and credibility. Undoubtedly, there will be disagreement about the proper methodology for evangelism. However, one must keep in mind that methodology is not evangelism, but rather a means to evangelize. The method must never be allowed to become an end in itself.

While preparing the final draft of these lectures, I used a carrel in the library at the Methodist Theological School in Ohio. Before going into the carrel, I would pass under a banner with this rather motivational thought on it: "Methodism: Holiness of Heart and Life."

The thought on that banner has been on my mind lately; for after all, isn't that what the Christian life is all about? It seems to me that regardless of the topic or the theme to be addressed, in the ultimate analysis, the Christian life is a matter of holiness of heart and life. This is the bottom line, is it not? This is pure Wesley, who taught us that happiness equals holiness, and holiness equals happiness. In more recent times a beloved mentor, Albert Outler (who delivered the 1971 Denman Lectures), issued a clarion call regarding the urgency of the "Third Great Awakening" and challenged us all to respond to the claim of God upon our lives. He spoke about the fact that, in the final analysis, the issue is holiness of heart and life, bringing together not just knowledge and vital piety but also grace and work, original sin and Christian perfection, justification and sanctification, evangelism and involvement in the issues of our world, word and deed. It takes a genius of a man—like John Wesley (for his time) and Outler (for our time)—to bring about this glorious blend of law and gospel that we so urgently need today.

When Outler spoke about "evangelism in the Wesleyan spirit,"[6] he did something else in that memorable Congress: He helped the participants transcend all theological labels. There were liberals present who forgot all about that label, and there were evangelicals who felt very

---

6 Discussed in *Evangelism and Theology in the Wesleyan Spirit*, by Albert C. Outler; © 1996 Discipleship Resources, Nashville, Tennessee.

much affirmed. And now we come to Kansas City in 1998 with a heartfelt prayer that this can happen again: no more labels! We must go forth from here with only one label: Christian. Our label means that we bring healing and wholeness together in our hearts and in our lives, in word and in deed. This I hope is the happy marriage of the personal and social dimensions of the gospel, which indeed belong together.

We need to come together and embrace one another, gathering under the banner of "the gospel as invitation." The gospel *is* invitation. God is an inviting God who says, "Come to the banquet; come to the feast—the fiesta—for my son was dead and is alive, was lost and is found" (Luke 15:23-24, adapted).

Obviously, we will differ in some of the semantics of evangelism. Some will call it "liberation," while others will speak about "deliverance." Some will talk about "healing and wholeness," while others will speak about the "integration of personality." Our methodology and terminology may differ, but we must all agree on the basic theological and biblical premise that "in Christ God was [and is] reconciling the world to himself...and entrusting the message of reconciliation to us" (2 Corinthians 5:19).

There is hope! We need to face the harsh realities of our time and strategize wisely, for we don't have the luxury of ignoring them. We must find a way to deal with these realities, inspired by an undying hope.

It is estimated that in the United States of America alone, there are more than seventy-four million unchurched people; of these, one out of three is between the ages of thirty-five and fifty-five. Many of these people have come to realize that life is more than just material things. Many of them are searching for meaning in life. As the baby boomers try to find fulfillment, we are presented with an unusual opportunity for evangelism, through regular worship services, small-group settings, or numerous other ways. This is a time to rethink our priorities and to use creative responses to new opportunities, as Alan Waltz has written. I agree with him that if we don't, the passage of time will determine the destiny of our denomination.[7]

The religiously unaffiliated people are the fastest-growing religious group in the United States of America. Islam is the fastest-growing form of religion in the United States.

---

7 Discussed in *To Proclaim the Faith*, by Alan K. Waltz (Abingdon Press, 1983); page 138.

While attending the meeting of the Academy for Evangelism in Theological Education, held at St. Paul's School of Theology in Kansas City, I went for a walk. As I stood on top of a hill overlooking the beautiful Kansas City skyline, I couldn't help but notice the cross on top of the steeple of the Kresge Chapel. There was a bird perched on the cross singing a song of praise. It was as though the bird were proclaiming to the whole world that there is something that can defeat the tragedy of evil and that the power of God overcomes even death. Likewise, we can sing over the desperate cries of the lonely voices in the city and proclaim that there is hope over despair for those who have lost vision and are disenchanted; that there is acceptance for those who feel rejected; that "whosoever will, may come"; and that the invitation is now extended again with the words made memorable by my friend Charles D. Whittle, "We must get back into the invitation business!"

We need to ask ourselves if what we are saying is clearly understood by our listeners. Are they getting it? Are we clear in what we are talking about? The message that is conveyed, either privately or publicly, must be grounded in the Scriptures as the will of God and be relevant to the needs of people today. We must interpret the message in a new way that is "seeker-friendly."

In these lectures, I intend to relate these principles to the life of the local church and affirm that the local church needs to be sensitive to what is happening in the world. The church also needs to make clear the message of love, as well as the invitation, "Come with us to Christ, and the church."

I know that the church has sometimes been labeled "an eight-track church in a CD world." We live in a highly technological, digital world. The question is, Can the church catch up with what is happening, without compromising its integrity?

How does one answer this question? Outler contends, "Zeal, passion, rhetorical overkill—none of these, nor all of them together, constitute the secret of effective evangelism."[8]

If this is true, the answer must emerge out of our struggle with both the contemporary scenario and the ancient and eternal truth of God. It is an answer guided by the Holy Spirit that addresses people where they are today.

8   From *Evangelism and Theology in the Wesleyan Spirit*, by Albert C. Outler; © 1996 Discipleship Resources, Nashville, Tennessee; page 19.

The following are some meaningful directives that could point to a resolution of dysfunctional situations in congregations—that is, paralyzing conditions that are deadly, such as conflict, negligence, or lethargy:

▲ Depend heavily upon God's abundant grace.

▲ Develop a true passion for "souls" (people).

▲ Be thoroughly informed and theologically aware.

▲ Use contemporary ways of communicating the gospel effectively.

▲ Use practical time-management devices in ministry.

▲ Think globally.

▲ Be willing to test parameters and assumptions and engage in meaningful dialogue with those who disagree.

▲ Learn to be a catalytic agent and thus speed the process of revitalization.

▲ Develop a positive vision that brings about a "can-do" attitude ("stick-to-itiveness").

▲ Be willing to move forward with non-traditional methodologies and be willing to test innovative strategies.

▲ Mobilize the laity into true discipleship.

▲ Use web sites on the Internet that provide helpful information.

When I write about "invitational evangelism," I do not necessarily mean some kind of invitation *system* in evangelism. This is an important concern. What I mean by invitational evangelism is an in-depth understanding of a basic tenet of the Christian faith that holds that the very nature of the gospel is invitational. This concept goes far beyond the matter of the number of people who go forward or sign a card.

Invitational evangelism takes seriously the reality of effective pastoral leadership. We are all vulnerable at this point, but the issue is clear: Unless we find ways to give priority to the issue of evangelism, it will not happen. Many believe that there is a crisis in the life of the church and that the crisis is partly the result of our inability to do effective marketing and cross-cultural communication. The question is, How are we going to revitalize the church? How are we going to be a truly evangelistic church that is true to the gospel and, at the same time, faithful in mission and ministry?

All the great preaching is of no avail unless the people are there to hear it. Therefore, there needs to be effective strategies to reach outsiders and to get them to come into the sanctuary. Once they are in the sanctuary, prayer is the most powerful vehicle to reach them. In addition, they need to have high expectations in order to respond to the gospel.

Invitational evangelism holds every individual in high regard. It does not violate the individual's personality or exploit his or her weaknesses. Invitational evangelism is done in the spirit of friendship and caring. We have to earn the right to talk to another person about Jesus Christ. This right is earned by first becoming true friends. It is indeed a travesty of the spirit of the gospel to reject those who are reluctant to respond to the gospel.

Invitational evangelism includes two basic elements: faith and repentance. They are mutually complementary, and out of their blend comes conversion (Romans 10:17).

There are many guidelines for becoming an invitational church. They supply material for further reflection and application in individual situations. Obviously we cannot afford the luxury of disregarding some traditional models. However, emerging models include some criteria that ensure greater credibility for the gospel in today's world. These criteria include the following:

▲ All people—clergy and laity alike—must share in ministry.
▲ Church leaders must intentionally plan programs that reflect a seven-day-a-week church.[9]
▲ Whatever "follow-up" program is planned must focus upon people and their needs.
▲ Whatever is done in the life of the church must be done with the importance of outreach in mind.
▲ The role of the pastor is primarily that of equipping the laity for ministry.
▲ Programs must be decentralized as much as possible.
▲ Small groups must be organized for the purpose of evangelism.
▲ The small groups or "cell" groups must set goals for reaching out to a given community, with a view to bringing people to faith in Christ and into membership in the church.
▲ It is of utmost importance to involve all believers in some kind of small-group experience.

9 Discussed in *The Seven-Day-a-Week Church*, by Lyle E. Schaller (Abingdon Press, 1992).

▲ It is also important to make sure that a small group engages in
some kind of social outreach and service.

▲ People in a small group need to have training in specific skills,
particularly in faith sharing.[10]

▲ Specific plans must be made to assimilate new members into the
church so that every new member will be active in at least one
small-group experience.

As mentioned earlier, Dr. Outler spoke to the Congress on Evangelism in New Orleans in January 1971. Some of you still remember his
marvelous Denman Lectures titled "Evangelism in the Wesleyan
Spirit."[11] It was at that time that he spoke with a powerful, prophetic
voice about the First and Second Great Awakenings, and his prayerful
hope for a Third Great Spiritual Awakening—perhaps within this century. We're about to come to the close of the century, and that Third
Great Awakening has not occurred, even though we have seen some
facets of it here and there (for example, the Promise Keepers and the
Charismatic Movement).

Some of us are still praying that the Third Great Spiritual Awakening will occur in this century or at the beginning of the twenty-first
century. Surely, it is sorely needed. But as Dr. Outler said, the Third
Great Awakening is going to be different from the First and Second
Great Awakenings. The changing times of which he spoke in the seventies demanded a different type of awakening and, needless to say,
the radically different scenario of the twenty-first century will require
an even more radically different expression of the awakening.

Paraphrasing some of his ideas, including some additional ones of
my own, it seems to me that the Third Great Awakening, whenever it
should occur, would have to include some, and preferably all, of the
following characteristics:

▲ It must be profoundly evangelical, with an emphasis on God's
sovereign grace in Christ.

▲ It must include a delicate balance between God's grace and
human response. (See Chapter Two on preaching for a response.)

10 Discussed in *Faith-Sharing: Dynamic Christian Witnessing by Invitation*, by H. Eddie Fox and George E. Morris (Discipleship Resources, 1996). Also discussed in *The Faith-Sharing Congregation: Developing a Strategy for the Congregation as Evangelist*, by Roger K. Swanson and Shirley F. Clement (Discipleship Resources, 1996).

11 The lectures have been reprinted and included in *Evangelism and Theology in the Wesleyan Spirit*, by Albert C. Outler (Discipleship Resources, 1996).

▲ It must include the essential elements of Christian nurture—such as prayer, Scripture reading, witnessing, serving others, and the observance of the sacraments—which is a lifelong process.

▲ It must maintain the centrality of prevenient grace that surrounds and anticipates every crisis, individually and collectively.

▲ It must call men and women to repentance and conversion, but also to be active participants of the body of Christ—the community of faith—and to enlistment as disciples of Jesus Christ.

▲ It must reconcile the polarities between knowledge and vital piety, personal and social gospel, traditional and contemporary evangelistic models, pastoral and prophetic ministry, outreach and nurture, academic competence and the practice of ministry and mission.

▲ It must let go of some of the excess baggage of the eighteenth and nineteenth centuries and recreate a whole new understanding of the evangelical and Wesleyan traditions as we minister to the postmodern mindset.

▲ It must include a powerful and intentional approach to witnessing by the laity.

Yes, we face a window of opportunity; and in the Congress on Evangelism, we must recover a vision of authentic evangelism and find a sense of direction, if evangelism is to be kept alive and vital in the life of our postmodern world. I would like to sound a clarion call for the gospel as a response to the challenging and puzzling issues facing evangelism in the twenty-first century.

The undergirding text for all the chapters in this book is taken from John 7:37, which reads, "On the last day of the festival, the great day, while Jesus was standing there, he cried out, 'Let anyone who is thirsty come to me.'"

Chapter One

Unexpected Invitation:

Toward a Theology for Evangelism

GOD'S INVITATION

I begin with an unforgettable story that was told by the late Bishop Robert Goodrich. A young girl did not know how to pray and decided instead to write a letter to God. She was in the midst of a crisis, so her letter was brief and to the point. "Dear God," she wrote, "I need you. But, O God, where are you?"

This question becomes the basis for my thinking about invitational evangelism, which seeks to answer the question asked by the young girl in the story. But it is not just her question; the same question is asked by every person around the world sometime in his or her life.

This chapter is based on the evangelical view that holds high the revealed sovereign grace of God through Jesus Christ. I believe that we need to maintain a dynamic equilibrium between God's grace and human response. It is my theological conviction that the doctrine of prevenient grace is fundamental to invitational evangelism. Prevenient grace surrounds us and anticipates every crisis that we experience. Even before we approach a person with the gospel, prevenient grace is already present in his or her life. Furthermore, I firmly believe that people cannot save themselves and that we are hopelessly lost without Christ.

In our better moments, we know that something is wrong. This is the human dilemma—the human predicament. Modern men and women must come to terms with their alienation from God, but they must also come to terms with the gift of grace. It is always possible to come to God, who alone gives meaning and purpose to our lives.

A theology of invitation attempts to address the human dilemma—the question of what's wrong with human life. In so doing, it is able to help overcome the tragedy of separation from God. In the final analysis, though, there is a miracle, not only of a changed heart but also of changing doubt into faith and fear into hope, and rejoicing in the glory of the risen Christ, who is Lord of all life.

Our son Paul, who is a pastor in Dallas, Texas, wrote in his newsletter an article based on "The Secret Garden," a Broadway musical.

> In the Broadway musical, "The Secret Garden," a young orphaned girl, adopted by her recently widowed uncle, meets with cold resistance when she tries to befriend him. But she persists, while at the same time taking an interest in the lush flower gardens in the yard of her new home. Thinking she might like to plant something herself, the young girl asks permission from her uncle: "I would like to plant a small garden of my own," she explains. "All I need is 'a bit of earth.'"
>
> Reluctantly, her uncle consents, in more ways than one. He grants her some room for planting in the yard, but also, over time, he begins to make room in his own heart for his niece's love. By the story's end his cold and bitter heart has warmed, and he is human again. All she asked for was "a bit of earth." And from it comes a garden.[12]

The prophet Isaiah spoke well when he looked forward to the day when "the wilderness and the dry land shall be glad, the desert shall rejoice and blossom; like the crocus it shall blossom abundantly, and rejoice with joy and singing" (Isaiah 35:1-2).

According to Luke, Jesus said,

> When you give a luncheon or a dinner, do not invite your friends or your brothers or your relatives or rich neighbors, in case they may invite you in return, and you would be repaid. But when you give a banquet, invite the poor, the crippled, the

---

12 Reported in *Good News From Munger Place United Methodist Church* newsletter, by Paul Escamilla; December 19, 1997. (Paul L. Escamilla is Senior Pastor at Walnut Hill UMC, Dallas, Texas.)

lame, and the blind. And you will be blessed, because they cannot repay you, for you will be repaid at the resurrection of the righteous.   (Luke 14:12-14)

This is a parable of the grace of God, whose message seems clear: No one attends the "great feast" unless invited by God. But, contrary to human practice and expectation, God invites *everyone*. Those who expect to be invited—those who believe it appropriate that they be invited—are the ones who make excuses. They, in effect, reject God's invitation. Those who were taught that they are not worthy of inclusion are the ones who accept God's invitation. God's invitation is always unexpected. Those who expect to be invited aren't open to God's invitation, because in assuming that they are worthy, they reject grace. Those who understand themselves to be unacceptable are open to receiving God's grace, astounding as that grace is.

Theology is important. What we believe about God and how we understand God matters, and it matters supremely. Theology deals with the nature of God—that is, with who God is and how he reveals himself. It also has to do with relationships: How does God relate to human beings, and how does he expect human beings to relate to him?

In both the Old and New Testaments, we discover that God is seeking us. Back in the Garden of Eden, God was seeking Adam and asking, "Where are you?" (Genesis 3:9). G. K. Chesterton, a well-known British writer and critic, has noted that the central idea of a large part of the Old Testament may be God's loneliness. Many other passages in the Old Testament reveal the nature of God as a seeking God. These passages portray a God who is not happy to be isolated from us and who wants us to come to him and to have fellowship with him.

There has been much discussion about a theology of evangelism. It seems as if in many quarters there is an excessive emphasis on the methodology of evangelism—with how to do evangelism. But what about the why of evangelism? What is our theological understanding of evangelism? Why "do evangelism" in the first place?

In this chapter I outline a theology of evangelism as invitation. That is, I am trying to focus primarily upon an understanding of the God who is always seeking, searching, inviting people to come to him or to return to him. I also refer to it as a theology of acceptance, in as much as I understand the meaning of Romans 5:8: "While we still were sinners Christ died for us." What this really means is that God's invitation is given to those who are lost, disenchanted, as well as many who find themselves in an alienated or estranged condition. It is as if the doors were open to everyone, especially those who are unworthy. A theology of acceptance says, "Come as you are; you are accepted now!"

We fear most the thought that God will not love us anymore because of our imperfections. Sometimes this is a carryover from childhood days when our parents instilled deeply within us the idea that if we behaved and did exactly what they expected us to do, we would have their love. If we didn't, there would be punishment and rejection. A theology of acceptance is a byproduct of our conviction that God will never stop loving us, regardless of what we do or fail to do. In other words, God's love is not determined by our behavior.

Let's define an invitational theology a bit more carefully. The content of such a theology would include the following:

▲ the gospel of "Christ, and him crucified" (1 Corinthians 2:2)
▲ the message of human sin and God's grace (John 3:16)
▲ the reality of human guilt and divine forgiveness (1 John 1:9)
▲ the new birth and the new life through the gift of the Holy Spirit (John 3:6-8)

These points bear some elaboration. First, there are many different Christologies in the New Testament. Our Christology obviously reflects our understanding of the person and work of Christ. I propose an evangelical Christology, based on a historic Christology, which proclaims Jesus as Savior and Lord. Second, a personal experience takes place in a person's life as a response to the proclamation of the good news. In turn, this experience is based on a theological tenet that affirms the reality of the risen Lord, who is now mysteriously present in that experience. Third, God grants salvation as a gift of grace; faith is the necessary human response that leads to a personal experience of God's grace.

John Wesley was not concerned about any kind of abstract exploration; rather, he was concerned about the personal appropriation of God's grace. This makes Christian experience itself a gift. Christian experience takes place when God and people connect.

CHRIST AND OUR THEOLOGY OF GRACE

An invitational theology is based on the understanding that the Bible is a book of redemption and that we extend God's invitation in the name of Jesus Christ because of God's love and mercy for every human being.

The word *evangelism* stems from the Greek word *evangelion*, which means good news. *Evangel* was translated into old English as *godspel*, meaning good news; it comes to us as *gospel*. So *evangel* and *gospel* both mean good news. *Evangelism*, then, is proclaiming the good news of what God has done for us in Jesus Christ.

Tradition has it that Martin Luther was frightened into pursuing holy orders. In the course of his training to become an Augustinian monk, he was plagued by a sense of his own unworthiness and his destiny of punishment. Apparently, Luther was a great problem to the confessors, because in his terror of God's judgment he would confess at great length. Upon leaving he would remember something else he should have confessed; he would hasten back to plead with the confessor to hear him again. In his works of penance, Luther so severely punished himself that he endangered his health and even his life.

This ingrained sense of the "terrifying God" was reinforced by the kind of theology in which Luther was trained. This theology emphasized both a demanding, wrathful deity and human beings' responsibility to exercise their willpower to obey and achieve righteousness.

Nevertheless, Luther completed his preparation and became a teacher. His diligent study of Scripture gradually led him to see the Christian faith in a profoundly different way. This recognition, though, came as a sudden experience. Luther described how a portion of the seventeenth verse of the first chapter of Romans leaped off the page, confronting him with Paul's affirmation that "the one who is righteous will live by faith."

Where Luther previously was convinced that God requires us to exercise our capacity to achieve righteousness in order to gain God's acceptance, he now realized that the gospel is "good news" precisely because God loves us in our sinfulness, despite our inability to be righteous and to earn God's approval. Trusting in God's graciousness makes it possible for us to become the creatures that God enables us to be.

The good news is a gift, undeserved and unmerited—that is, it is grace. We are "saved" by grace received in faith.

All these words are tricky. The word *faith* was commonly understood in Luther's time as intellectual assent to the doctrines of the church, and many continue to understand it in that way today. Luther argued that this was wrong, and that faith has the character of trust (*fides*). Faith was not just an act of intellect but of the whole self. Our problem is our fear of trusting in the One who was, and is, revealed in Jesus Christ.

> But now, apart from law, the righteousness of God has been disclosed, and is attested by the law and the prophets, the righteousness of God through faith in Jesus Christ for all who believe. For there is no distinction, since all have sinned and fall short of the glory of God; they are now justified by his grace as a gift. (Romans 3:21-24)

Unless we change our understanding of *faith* from intellectual assent to personal trust, we can easily fall into the trap (from which Luther escaped) of supposing that *justification by faith* means that God will approve of us only if we exercise our willpower to make ourselves believe (give intellectual assent to) the Christian teachings. But this is the reverse of Luther's teaching, for it makes the act of believing into a "good work" deserving God's approval.

It helps to note that Luther altered not only his understanding of faith but also his view of sin—the human problem in relating to God. From a legalistic and "works righteousness" viewpoint, sin is understood as willful disobedience. In this view, the implicit assumption is that we humans are naturally capable of being and doing what God requires of us. In contrast, Luther became convinced that sin is the absence of faith. Insofar as we do not trust in God, accepting God's free gift, we are alienated from God and trapped in hearts "curved in" upon themselves. We are not able to love, which is to say that we are not able to live in accordance with God's will. It is only in trusting in God's grace that we are enabled to fulfill God's intentions. God does not demand a righteousness we cannot fulfill; instead, God offers the gift that makes it possible for us to begin to grow in grace and become righteous.

The twentieth-century theologian Paul Tillich argued that we may better grasp the basis of growing in grace if we recognize that faith is not just trusting in God but letting God take a hold of our lives. Tillich was emphasizing his conviction that the primary agent in the faith relationship is God, not us.

This is consistent with Tillich's further suggestion that we should not speak of "justification by faith," which easily invites the misunderstanding of faith as a "good work"; rather, we should affirm that we are justified by grace through faith.

It is this focus upon the grace of God, who accepts the unacceptable, that was at the heart of Luther's revolution and the beginning of the Protestant church. One may note that in Germany the established Protestant church is not called Protestant, but Evangelical. This notes that the church is founded on the "good news." I must hasten to add that, in our time, "evangelical" does not serve to distinguish Protestants from Roman Catholics, for many prominent Roman Catholic theologians also teach that it is by grace that we are saved, and thus concur with Luther's understanding of faith.

This, then, is the "evangel," the good news: God is grace; grace is sovereign. Nothing "will be able to separate us from the love of God in Christ Jesus our Lord" (Romans 8:39).

In the larger context of Jesus' parable of the Great Feast, we see that it is God who invites; and for us Christians, it is Jesus Christ through whom God extends the divine invitation. Leonard Sweet describes God's invitation this way:

> Jesus does not say, "Get your affairs straightened out, and then I'll eat with you." Jesus does not say, "You want to come to my table? Then shape up." Jesus eats with people in the midst of their brokenness, people that good people, then as today, do not find acceptable. Jesus identifies with people precisely where they are hurting most and fearing most and failing most. Jesus eats with the good, the bad, and the both.[13]

Sweet's comment "people that good people, then as today, do not find acceptable" reflects the reality—in Jesus' parable as well as today—that many people make excuses and do not accept God's invitation. If we wonder why anyone would reject an invitation to a great banquet, we can all think of what to us are reasonable answers; for we all—at one time or another—have probably done just that. But it may

---

13 From *The Jesus Prescription for a Healthy Life*, by Leonard Sweet; © 1996 Abingdon Press; page 148. Used by permission.

seem much more difficult to explain why anyone would reject God's invitation.

THE REJECTION OF INVITATIONAL PREACHING

The reluctance to risk trusting in God in the face of martyrdom, persecution, sacrifice, criticism, or even inconvenience illustrates the human condition in general. Christian faith understands that we humans were created by Love for love, but love is not something that can be caused or coerced. To accept love and to love require risk and responsibility, so God created us with the gift of the possibility of loving. Part of this possibility lies in the fact that we are self-reflective creatures. We are consciously aware of ourselves, and this makes possible virtually all of the other characteristics that we identify as human: sociality, linguisticality, humor, morality, and so forth. It also means that we enter life both as a species and as individuals with a developing awareness of our finitude. We come to know that we are mortal, that we need others, that it is not certain that our lives have any meaning. So, to be finite and self-conscious is to feel threatened; indeed, it is to feel anxious.

Hence, the inevitable basic human motivation is anxious self-protectiveness, with hearts "curved in" upon themselves, as Luther said. In this condition we seek security. We struggle to build structures and relationships that will ward off the threats of death, loneliness, meaninglessness, and guilt. Because we do so motivated by anxious self-centeredness, these security mechanisms become sources of alienation. Racism, for example, is a futile effort to affirm one's own value by seeing those who are different as being of less value. The same can be said for sexism, nationalism, ageism, and all the other invidious human prejudices. If the tax collectors, the poor, and the outcasts are going to be at the banquet, we don't want to be there.[14]

In theological terms, we are talking of *idolatry*; for that term really means trusting, or finding our deepest security, in anything other than God. In some ways it is easier to trust in money or power. These things are tangible; God isn't. Affirming other people is clearer to us than God's grace. So we follow many strategies for gaining friendships and the approval of our fellow human beings (the ones we identify with),

14 I acknowledge the highly helpful insights that Dr. Jeffrey Hopper shared with me about this topic.

and we build relationships founded on mutual anxiety and self-centered need. In these and many other ways, we deceive ourselves, compound our basic problem, and avoid the risk of trusting in grace.

This makes it clear why so many people reject God's invitation. In order to trust in grace and allow ourselves to be grasped by the Holy Spirit, we must let go of all our security structures. This goes directly against our most basic motivation: to rely on ourselves. What could be more frightening than trusting in God's grace? Grace can't be possessed, controlled, or manipulated—though we surely try to do all of these things. Grace can't be proven or demonstrated scientifically. It can't be objectively established beyond a reasonable doubt. We have to let go of the side of the pool and trust the water to hold us up.

Our inevitable captivity to anxious self-centeredness makes it most difficult for us to come to trust in God. We keep wanting God to do things that will assure us both of his reality and of his goodness. We want evidence. Yet, this shows only that we don't trust in God, but we would trust in evidence. Some people have been able to delude themselves into believing that they have proof of God's reality and of God's favor. But evidence is always finite, so it could establish only finite conclusions. The God of Jesus Christ and biblical faith transcends all such limitations. Were that not so, we could not appropriately have faith in God.

THE SALVATION OFFERED

How, then, is it possible for us to escape from the estrangement in which our anxious self-centeredness holds us? The answer Christian faith gives is that God has overcome our alienation in Jesus Christ.

Historically, the Christian faith has affirmed that through Jesus—whom we call the Christ—God has wrought our salvation and has overcome our alienation from God, from ourselves, and from our neighbors. As Saint Paul says, "in Christ God was reconciling the world to himself" (2 Corinthians 5:19). But just how is this act of reconciliation to be understood? Throughout the history of the church, there has never been an official ecumenical declaration (or dogma) answering this question, although many explanations have been proposed. Some groups within the church have insisted that one explanation or another *must* be accepted, thus making doctrinal correctness a condition of salvation, and thereby rejecting grace. But the Christian church as a whole has shown wisdom in refusing to make any such requirement.

Each of the theories of atonement is a metaphor expressing for some people, or for a particular cultural setting, something of the experience of having been brought to faith and reconciled to God. This is done in response to the church's witness that we have been "graced" by God in and through Jesus Christ, and that it is therefore in him that we see both the reality of God-for-us and what God would enable us to be. There are still among us those who would declare that only their preferred theory of Christ's saving work is acceptable, and that those who don't agree with them are not people of faith and are therefore excluded from God's kingdom. This hardly conveys "good news."

It is surely useful to continue to grapple with our desire to understand more clearly Christ's saving work in order that we may more adequately proclaim it; but if we cannot do our debating in love, our witness will contradict our profession of faith. We would do well to recall Jesus' answer when John reported to Jesus that he and the other disciples tried to stop an exorcist (who was not one of the twelve apostles) from casting out demons in Jesus' name. Jesus said, "Do not stop him; for no one who does a deed of power in my name will be able soon afterward to speak evil of me. Whoever is not against us is for us" (Mark 9:39-40).

In faith, we know that "in Christ God was reconciling the world to himself" (2 Corinthians 5:19). For we have been reconciled, we have seen the grace of God in Jesus Christ, we have been set free from captivity, and we have been grasped by God's Spirit and enabled to grow in peace.

In the Scriptures, Christians find Christ manifested in creation, in the Fall, redemption, and consummation. Christ incarnate becomes the basis for meaningful human existence, in the past as well as in the future. Jesus Christ lived, died, and conquered death. He alone represents our hope in life and in death, in this world and in the world to come. Jesus Christ is Lord and Redeemer, King of Kings, and victorious over the power of death (1 Corinthians 15:26).

With historic Christianity, an invitational theology highlights the centrality of the person and work of Christ as Savior. It holds that the power of the saving grace of God through Jesus Christ should become functional in the life of a person. A historic Christology emphasizes both the full humanity and the full divinity of Christ, as well as his power to save.

In his sermon "Salvation by Faith," John Wesley presented the meaning of justification:

> This then is the salvation which is through faith, even in the present world: a salvation from sin, and the consequences of sin, both often expressed in the word *justification*; which, taken in the largest sense, implies a deliverance from guilt and punishment, by the atonement of Christ actually applied to the soul of the sinner now believing on him, and a deliverance from the whole body of sin, through Christ formed in his heart. So that he who is thus justified, or saved by faith, is indeed born again.[15]

Of course, the problem that we encounter with the word *salvation* is that it is a worn-out term. It is found in so many sermons, hymns, and liturgies. While the term is central to the New Testament message, it has unfortunately lost much of its power in our day. The term *salvus* means to heal, to make whole. Using synonyms of the term can help people today understand the meaning of salvation: Salvation is healing, liberation, being set free. It is reunion; it is responding to the invitation to come and drink of the living waters (John 4:10).

An invitational theology begins by calling the church to repentance. It has been said before that there is no question that God can convert the world; rather, the question is, Can God convert the church? Quite frequently the church is unaware of the need for repentance and conversion. But the place for the church to begin is to repent of its sins of commission as well as its sins of omission. For example:

▲ The church has often forgotten about the oppressed.
▲ The church has ignored the cry of the poor.
▲ The church has not always been there for others.
▲ The church in its affluence has not always been mindful of the sacrifice of others that made its affluence possible.

THE WORK OF THE SPIRIT AND THE HUMAN CONDITION

The theology of invitation holds that the Holy Spirit is indeed the Evangelizer. The power of the Holy Spirit is manifested through the

---

15 From "Salvation by Faith," a sermon by John Wesley, as quoted in *Practical Divinity: Theology in the Wesleyan Tradition*, by Thomas A. Langford; © 1983 Abingdon Press; page 29. Used by permission.

preaching of the Word of God. The person of the Holy Spirit is the most powerful resource we have for dealing with the awful condition of sinfulness and alienation. The Holy Spirit bridges the gap of separation between God and humanity and reaches out to the listener in his or her existential condition. A historic Christology teaches that the encounter with Jesus Christ is just as real today as it was during the days of his flesh. It holds that Christ is spiritually present through the Holy Spirit and that his presence is manifested through preaching as well as other acts of witness and service.

Before I talk about the work of the Holy Spirit, I want to elaborate on the human condition alluded to earlier in this chapter. All of us are aware of the reality of the human predicament. There is a restless discontent in the hearts of men and women today. Many of them have come to feel that life is meaningless. Others affirm with Albert Camus, the well-known French writer and philosopher, that life is absurd.

How can we understand the human condition? To be able to extend God's invitation meaningfully, it is essential that we have a clear understanding of the human condition. To understand it, all we have to do is read Genesis again—or perhaps read it with new eyes—and be grasped by the reality of the awful alienation that took place on the part of Adam, who disobeyed God and placed blame on someone else.

Then there is the story of pride as manifested in Cain, to be repeated later in the event of the Flood. This was followed by the Tower of Babel, which became a dramatic symbol of human arrogance. As someone has said, "Babel became a babble." Alienated from one another, people were unable to relate meaningfully.

In this brief summary of the story of the human condition, Adam symbolizes the human being; therefore, his story is the story of every person at sometime in his or her life. The consequences of Adam's initial disobedience and of "original sin" or human depravity manifest themselves in our world today.

God created men and women as free beings, but they tend to misuse their freedom. We today can identify with misuse of freedom—it is our predicament also. Note the disillusionment and brokenness, insecurity and fear, selfishness, envy, jealousy, and other negative emotions.

Since sin is a universal condition, we need to think first of sin in the singular before we think about "sins." The concept of original sin or humanity's fallen state may sound difficult, but all it refers to is human self-centeredness and idolatry; that is, it has to do with people worshiping something other than God—a god.

The human condition means disorder in—the perversion of—human life everywhere. As a result of their disobedience and pride, humans create chaos out of order. This excessive assertiveness—this rebellion against God—is the source of many other problems that we find in our contemporary society. An esteemed theologian once wrote that when people realize that they are not the center of the world and then try to find an answer to their dilemma, they will discover that the answer lies in God's love revealed by Christ in his life and death. This is the foundation of the theology of invitation: Christ comes into our lives as the only one who can deliver us.

The human predicament is sometimes identified as the restlessness of the human heart. There is an emptiness within. People try to find fulfillment in material things. They secure all kinds of comforts in their homes, to no avail. They get promotions, to no avail. They travel all over the world, to no avail. They acquire fame and recognition, to no avail. Nothing seems to satisfy the hunger of the human heart.

This built-in need in every person—without exception—sets the agenda for evangelism. Evangelism is the inevitable answer to the universal human condition. The human dilemma of meaninglessness and rebellion against God can receive an answer only by a heart receptive to the grace of God.

Invitational theology addresses the reality of sin (not "sins") in the lives of people. In place of despair and helplessness, invitational theology offers joy and life abundant through repentance and forgiveness. Forgiveness opens our eyes to the gift that God is constantly offering to everyone.

The theology of invitation assumes that human beings have a need for God; they are separated from God; they are homeless; they are spiritually hungry. Invitational theology is a way of inviting people to come home to God, to the native land of the soul. The invitation can be accepted or rejected, for God created men and women to be free.

It is a matter of choice, but ample experience demonstrates that to reject the invitation means misery and pain. However, to accept the invitation means joy and peace and celebration; after all, it means to come to the feast—the "fiesta." This is what invitational evangelism is all about.

Sometimes people say that they want religion, not theology. They say, "Give us the simple gospel without any theological jargon." Yet, we quickly realize that it is virtually impossible to separate religion from theology. As theologians—and all of us are theologians—we are entrusted with the sublime task of using the intellectual gifts that God has given us to sort out the nature and purpose of God. Once we understand the nature of God as revealed supremely through Jesus Christ, we are in a position to think about how God is in the business of constantly inviting men and women to come to him.

The main problem, which becomes a real obstacle to any kind of evangelistic activity, is to face the reality of resistance and rebellion on the part of the person who needs God. We cannot afford to ignore this reality, and we must remember that even in the midst of resistance and rebellion, God continues to extend the invitation.

Even those who have accepted God's invitation have dark areas in their souls, places they will not allow God's grace to penetrate and illuminate. Frequently, these people have not surrendered their lives completely to God. Human pride will not allow Christ to be Lord of every aspect of our lives; therefore, it is always possible to surrender our lives more fully to God.

The choice is ours. As Wesleyans, we believe that people have the choice to either accept or reject God's invitation. Those who decide to reject the invitation make a decision to separate themselves from God's love, which is what hell is. Those who decide to leave God out of their lives lead a hellish existence. By leading self-centered lives, people make life miserable—both for themselves and for everyone around them. Separating from God is the most awful decision a person can make, for he of she chooses to be less than what God has intended him or her to be.

What is the role of the Holy Spirit in drawing people to God? Invitational theology is based on the conviction that through the Holy Spirit, God continues to extend the invitation, even to those who have rejected God and have hardened their hearts. God continues to knock at the door of their hearts, fully aware that the lock is found always on the inside. Sometimes God's invitation comes through a time of silent meditation. At other times, it reaches us through the genuine witness of other people. Sometimes God's invitation comes in the form of a word or sentence we read. On other occasions, God invites us in the midst of pain or tragedy. At still other times, it is precisely through the joy of human fulfillment that the whispering voice is heard and we hearken to God's voice.

THE PRIMACY OF GOD'S LOVE

An invitational theology is founded upon the premise of love. That love is what prompts and governs our evangelistic work. It is genuine care—as opposed to hot-headed zeal—for those whom we are trying to reach. The hot-headed kind of zeal is inappropriate, both in the pulpit and on a personal level.

God has a purpose for the life of every person and is concerned and interested in the outcome of that purpose. This is what brings hope to the human predicament. God's providence applies to all men and women in all kinds of circumstances. God is still fighting to bring good out of every experience in life (Romans 8:28).

Of all the divine attributes, God's love is perhaps the most important. "We love [God] because he first loved us" (1 John 4:19). God calls us one by one to respond to his ceaseless invitation. While we do not have to think of God in anthropomorphic (human) terms, we know that God has human-like attributes; therefore, we need to use those terms to understand what God is like.

Christians hold that God is a person in the sense that God is personal. God is a spirit, immeasurable, eternal, and infinite; at the same time, God knows and cares about the world. God came to heal the inner brokenness of sins, to cleanse us from fear and anxiety—but especially from sin. God desires to redeem us from sin and death, for he has brought us new, abundant, and eternal life.

An invitational theology is thus based on a theology of grace, and grace alone. How can we possibly define grace except to say that it is God's favor—always unmerited, unconditional, accepting? Grace makes possible a renewed relationship with God. Grace is a gift that keeps on giving. As prevenient, grace is already present in everyone's heart even before he or she decides to accept that grace. Grace is God in action; and it is love manifested in a thousand ways. It is amazing!

The theology of invitation also takes seriously the utmost importance of the church as the body of Christ. The church is not only the place where God's invitation is extended but also an environment where people who have accepted the invitation can grow. When the church provides nurture through Word and sacrament, it empowers converts to go forth in witness and service to the whole world. The church as a community of faith stands as a living witness to God's revelation in Jesus Christ. It is in the church where the process of sanctification takes place.

It is important for us to understand the importance of a sound ecclesiology—that is, an understanding of the nature and mission of the church. The church is a divine creation. Christ is the Lord of the church. The church belongs to God and will be preserved until the end of time. Sometimes we forget this fact; at other times, we need to be reminded that there is nothing that can ultimately destroy the church. God sustains the church forever.

Invitational theology motivates individuals and churches to be in mission, to bring the truth of God's redemptive act to every person in the whole world. The goal is that people will accept the good news and the abundant life that Christ offers, and then, on their part, extend God's invitation to others, both as individuals and as a church. In this way, the church becomes an invitational or evangelistic church—a missionary church. Christians who do not extend the invitation to come to Christ and who do not share the good news are failing in their commitment to fulfill the Great Commission. There is a well-known saying that says: "If you are not a missionary, you are a mission field." If a church is not extending its outreach to the lost, it becomes self-centered and ingrown, and it begins to decline.

Both in our individual lives and in the church, the Holy Spirit heals our wounds, renews our strength, washes away guilt, touches our hearts and wills, brings fire to our souls, and guides our steps rightly.

The Holy Spirit has unfortunately been misunderstood by many church leaders; they consider the Holy Spirit an abstract concept, too mysterious to understand.

An invitational theology affirms just the opposite: the role of the Holy Spirit has to do with daily life. The Spirit is a powerful source of inspiration and strength, which gives us the motivation and courage to witness and to love others unselfishly. The Spirit guides us in the midst of confusion, gives us peace in the midst of turmoil, provides power to preach God's Word, enlightens our consciences, gives clear direction for our lives, and is the source of all the fruits of the Spirit (Galatians 5:22). That is why we need daily to pray, "Come, Holy Spirit!"

Without the Holy Spirit, we as the body of Christ don't have the power to extend God's invitation. Without the Holy Spirit, our work is to no avail. Without the Holy Spirit, we do not have any authority to preach or to witness. Without the Holy Spirit, our theology is mere words without meaning.

On the other hand, with the Holy Spirit in our lives, we are constantly being renewed. The Holy Spirit penetrates into the ordinary moments of our lives. The mystery of the future is clarified with a new vision because we know that the Holy Spirit is at work. The power of the Holy Spirit enables us to overcome all of the obstacles that we encounter along the way, and enables the church to march forward like an army with banners, with supernatural power and a compelling dynamic that becomes an inevitable force.

GIFT AND MYSTERY

In *Hopeful Imagination: Prophetic Voices in Exile*, Walter Brueggemann reminds us that the poet in exile issues a call for his people to come home. For Brueggemann, the church in North America is similarly summoned to return home from exile.[16] The gospel announces its message that we may go home. The gospel defines *home*, not in terms of the dominant value system, but rather as a kingdom of love, justice, peace, and freedom.

Pope John Paul II selected a rather intriguing title for his autobiography: *Gift and Mystery: On the Fiftieth Anniversary of My Priestly Ordination*.[17] Three things in the book excited me a great deal. First, the title. My own life has been one of gift and mystery. All that I am,

---

16 Discussed in *Hopeful Imagination: Prophetic Voices in Exile*, by Walter Brueggemann (Fortress Press, 1986).
17 *Gift and Mystery: On the Fiftieth Anniversary of My Priestly Ordination*, by Pope John Paul II (Doubleday, 1996).

all that I have attained, is a gift—a gift of grace. Countless numbers of people have brought me untold gifts.

Second, the word *mystery*. My whole life has been a mystery. The sequence of events, doors that were opened—not to mention marvelous "coincidences"—are beyond description. Some would indeed call all this mere coincidence, but I call it God's leading. My life continues to be a mystery of grace. Pope John Paul's suggestive title has universal application, for all of us would surely agree that our lives have been ones of gift and mystery.

Third, toward the end of the book, the Pope writes about the need to offer Christ to people who are thirsty. Does this sound familiar? This is precisely what John Wesley told Francis Asbury as Asbury was leaving on a journey to America. Wesley said to Asbury, "Offer them Christ." The great artist Kenneth Wyatt has created a magnificent painting of that farewell event, a painting found in many churches across our land.

To me, this is *the* question: What else but Christ can we offer people? What else can we give to men and women who are hungry and thirsty? What else can we say to those who are lost in the jungle of our postmodern world? What else can we offer those who are confused and perplexed and disenchanted with life and with the church? What else can we offer the sin-sick soul? We offer only one thing: God's remedy—Christ!

On the way back from attending the Oxford Institute of Methodist Theological Studies in the summer of 1997, I read Donald English's book *An Evangelical Theology of Preaching*.[18] One chapter is titled "Atonement, Repentance, and Conversion"; familiar enough words, but they could be difficult for postmoderns to understand unless we explain them. But what caught my attention was the subtitle: "If This Is the Solution, What Is the Problem?" Indeed, before we talk about evangelism, we need to talk about the problem: the human condition. As God's initiative, evangelism must be directed precisely to the fragmented, sinful soul of human beings—to address the problem. Without repentance and faith in Christ, the problem of the human soul will not be resolved. Only repentance and faith can address the awesome emptiness of the human heart and the seemingly incurable sickness of

18 *An Evangelical Theology of Preaching*, by Donald English (Abingdon Press, 1996).

the soul. It is said that one of the Spanish conquerors, on coming to the New World in search for gold, said, "My sickness cannot be cured by all the gold and all the silver. The sickness that I have is the sickness of the soul."

Undoubtedly, there are many eloquent preachers across the United States of America. However, after some of their sermons one could probably remark, "You've preached a great sermon, but you forgot to extend the invitation!" There are many places where the harvest is ripe for the invitation, but it is never extended. Why don't we extend the invitation? We cannot afford the luxury of being ambivalent or ambiguous about this issue. People need to set their hearts right with God!

Many people in the pews of our congregations have steady jobs, decent salaries, and comfortable homes, but they live under constant pressure, stress, and burnout. They have trouble meeting the demands and expectations of their jobs and their families. Suddenly, when they realize that their lives and families are falling apart, they ask, "What went wrong?" They have three television sets and hold professional and managerial positions, but their lives are empty.

Invitational evangelism holds that it is the person in the pulpit who must answer the question about what went wrong. There should be an invitational approach, not just to visitors to the church but also to members who need a new and revitalizing experience with Christ. It has been said that the question isn't, How can God convert the world? The question, as stated earlier, is, How is God going to convert the church? Significant numbers of people in average congregations are not converted. To make matters worse, at least fifty percent of adults who join mainline denominations become inactive during their first year as members, according to Suzanne G. Braden.[19]

I believe that the answer to the crisis in evangelism does not lie in innovative programs, or in just trying harder. The nature of the crisis is much deeper—it is spiritual! That is why both pastors and laypeople need to be empowered by the Holy Spirit and catch the vision of an inviting God, so that we may go about the business of extending the invitation unashamedly. Jesus said to the disciples, "But you will receive power when the Holy Spirit has come upon you; and you will be my witnesses" (Acts 1:8).

19 Discussed in *The First Year: Incorporating New Members*, by Suzanne G. Braden (Discipleship Resources, 1987); page vii.

All of us need to know the statistics and take them seriously, but the deeper spiritual problem must be addressed. Statistics are symptomatic of the fact that there is something wrong in our relationship with God.

A woman recently said, "I want to go back to serious Bible study and attend a prayer group regularly. I don't want any more abstract homilies that have nothing to do with my life." If she's right, that is a serious matter for us all to consider.

If we were to take the "spiritual pulse" of most local churches, we would conclude that, for the most part, they are self-centered and interested only in institutional survival. They don't seem to care much about the outsider. They are complacent, and most of them have never even heard of invitational evangelism, much less try to practice it. However, there are churches across the land and overseas that are truly alive and engaged in ongoing evangelistic activities.

Questions for Reflection

1. Describe your own theology of evangelism. How does it agree or disagree with the understanding of "invitational theology" that is outlined in this chapter?
2. If you were to write a comprehensive definition of *evangelism*, what would the definition be?
3. What insights about evangelism can you learn from theological positions, such as liberation theology?
4. In what ways do you appropriate and share the good news in the place where you live, work, and play?
5. What does it mean to reflect theology on a specific evangelistic program?

Chapter Two

Invitational Preaching in the Twenty- First Century:

Preaching for a Response

THE CONTEXT OF OUR PREACHING TODAY

People today are searching for something to fill a void in their souls, an emptiness in their lives. Many are fed up with sexual promiscuity, alcohol and drugs, depression, and other aspects of our highly permissive society. Many want to know what the gospel has to offer. At issue is how to communicate the gospel to the modern, secularized mind in a way that makes sense to men and women, without compromising and abandoning the fundamental tenets of our faith. In this chapter, I contend that invitational preaching is well suited to accomplishing that task. After outlining the context of preaching in our day, I provide a general definition of invitational preaching; then I discuss in detail the role of the preacher, his or her message, and how to deliver the message so that it may have an impact in contemporary society.

The discussion to follow is based on the basic assumption that there is still *hope*, despite the bewildering ambivalence in which we find ourselves as a church. In the endeavor to deliver a message of hope, one must appropriate whatever wisdom may be found in secular culture (secular literature, science, and philosophy) and "plunder the

Egyptians" (Exodus 12:18-36); in this way, we can enhance the effectiveness of our preaching for a response.

Dr. Albert Outler is right when he says: "It is, therefore, a baffling time, a difficult time in which to proclaim the good news of God in Christ as credible and relevant." He adds:

> And yet—although our circumstances are radically different from Wesley's—it is just exactly the sort of crisis that he would have tried heroically to comprehend, confident that the perennial gospel still offers to us in the twentieth century the same eternal truth and hope he himself had proved it had for eighteenth century Englishmen: not only the lively hope of *heaven*, but also a credible hope for a meaningful life in *this* age (and any age) whatever its crises between theology and culture.[20]

Outler helps us all to understand the contemporary situation when he states:

> Human life must be lived in and by grace or else it will be lived gracelessly and ungraciously and death will find us not only vulnerable but literally hopeless. Autonomous humanity is foredoomed to hollow triumphs—to aspirations forever thwarted, to victories that wreak havoc and that leave the victors still unfulfilled.[21]

In the midst of the spiritual chaos of our contemporary world, there is indeed a desperate need for the type of preaching that provides genuine spirituality and that, at the same time, enables women and men to rediscover the meaning of comfort, joy, peace, mercy, and especially forgiveness. Thus, we have the need for what I call "invitational preaching"—preaching for a response.

We all know that every Sunday there are boring sermons preached everywhere. Likewise, there are meaningless sermons, irrelevant sermons, dead sermons, and so forth. In contrast, a sermon based on the principles of invitational preaching is alive, enthusiastic, scriptural, and based on unspoken human need.

Invitational preaching is not necessarily a new kind of preaching. As a matter of fact, it has existed since the beginning of the ministry of

20 From *Evangelism and Theology in the Wesleyan Spirit*, by Albert C. Outler; © 1996 Discipleship Resources, Nashville, Tennessee; page 76.
21 From *Evangelism and Theology in the Wesleyan Spirit*, by Albert C. Outler; © 1996 Discipleship Resources, Nashville, Tennessee; page 113.

Jesus, when he first issued the call and *invited* his disciples to come and follow him (Matthew 4:19; Mark 1:17). The same happens in Matthew 11:28, when Jesus issues a call to all who are weary and heavy-laden to come to him. Invitational preaching is rather obvious in John 7:37-38, when Jesus said in a loud voice on the last day of the feast, "Let anyone who is thirsty come to me, and let the one who believes in me drink."

We find this type of invitational preaching in the pages of the Old Testament as well. For instance, the prophet Isaiah extends an invitation by saying, "Everyone who thirsts, come to the waters" (Isaiah 55:1).

The fundamental question during John Wesley's time (as well as our time) was, "Who will rescue me from this body of death?" (Romans 7:24). The answer Wesley gave was, "Christ, and him crucified" (1 Corinthians 2:2).

The seed of what is broadly speaking called "evangelical preaching" is found in John Wesley's "heart-warming experience" at Aldersgate; for this experience led Wesley to proclaim the gospel in a particular way and with a particular emphasis. The first fruits of evangelical preaching were nourished on English soil. In America, that seed seems to have grown even more luxuriantly than in England; it branched out into more permutations as it adapted to new soils and climates. What I am calling "invitational preaching" is one of the adaptations of evangelical preaching.

Generally, among evangelicals the gospel is spread through preaching; therefore, the preacher is of paramount importance. The gospel is preached to win converts or to invite people to make other significant decisions. Ideally, the preacher preaches with passionate intensity, because he or she has been called by God, and consequently feels as compelled to preach as did Saint Paul, who cried, "Woe to me if I do not proclaim the gospel!" (1 Corinthians 9:16). Ideally, the evangelical preacher is anointed by the grace of God with the power of the Holy Spirit, as was Peter after Pentecost when he preached to a huge crowd and gained three thousand converts (Acts 2:41).

It is important to understand the term *evangelical* properly. It needs to be redefined over and over in order that we may appropriate the rich evangelical tradition and heritage. Preachers who are thought of as "evangelical" generally share the ideals mentioned above. To a certain extent, their preaching all share qualities described with terms like *grace-filled, anointed, Spirit-filled, charismatic,* and *invitational.*

THE NATURE OF INVITATIONAL PREACHING

Let us now consider evangelical preaching in a stricter sense than it was used in the previous section. As stated earlier, the main thrust of evangelical preaching is to win converts. To be sure, it is a great joy for any preacher when someone is persuaded to become a Christian by his or her sermon. Dr. Charles Brown, the former Dean of Yale Divinity School, wrote that following a response to the invitation when he preached his first sermon, he could not keep from crying because of the joy of serving Christ as a minister. However, when success and failure are measured by the number of converts, the preacher is tempted to use manipulative techniques to persuade some people to make a decision; or the preacher is tempted to regard a sermon as a failure if no one is converted as a consequence. By contrast, the dedicated invitational preacher will always bear in mind a point made by Alan Walker: Conversions are in the hands of God and the Holy Spirit, who alone do the evangelizing.[22]

Sermons need ample preparation. Times of prayer and meditation can never replace our responsibility to do adequate preparation for what we are going to preach about. We need to be thoroughly saturated with the heart of the text or passage. We need to be thoroughly aware of the need of people so that by the time we come to the pulpit, the grace of God may flow abundantly with charisma, power, vitality, and winsomeness. There should be a radiance in our demeanor that is obvious to all.

Many of us preachers fall into the trap of self-condemnation and self-hate. We have become emotionally drained as a result of overfatigue, and have overloaded our bodies. At times there is a hidden hostility within us; at other times we are disappointed and angry with God. We wonder why God doesn't intervene to bring about a perfect set of circumstances. In the winter of our discontent, we experience the inevitable curse of discouragement and failure. Invitational preaching? No way!

22 Discussed in *Standing Up to Preach: The Art of Evangelical Preaching,* by Alan Walker (Discipleship Resources, 1983); page 62.

What is the way out? There are no simple answers; any simplistic formulas are simply clichés—they sound good but do not actually work. To help someone move from despondency and despair to a renewed sense of vitality in the pulpit and to authentic invitational preaching, let me suggest the following: First, invitational preaching is based on the fact that we are earthen vessels—that even though our "outer nature is wasting away, our inner nature is being renewed" every day (2 Corinthians 4:16). Second, invitational, charismatic, and anointed preaching is successful when there is a climate of high expectation on the part of the congregation. The order of worship sets the stage for the effective proclamation of the Word.

PREACHING AND THE CONGREGATION'S LIFE

Whatever your personal theology and understanding of prayer may be, one thing is for sure: God answers prayer, sometimes in the most unexpected and amazing ways.

Think about the amazing impact that corporate prayer would have on you as a preacher. Think of the miracles that would happen if everyone in the congregation would pray silently for you as you preach. Think of how powerful it would be if people would keep thinking, *Lord, what do you want me to do about this?* Or, *Lord, I would like to take a step forward today.* Or, *You know my problem and you know my need. What is the sermon saying to me about my need?* And then for people to silently respond, *God, use me, your messenger, as a vehicle of your purpose for the sake of my life and the life of the world.* Or, *Lord, anoint the preacher with the power of the Holy Spirit.* Such a "silent conspiracy of prayer" will revolutionize the preaching as well as people's response to the preaching. Of all the compliments to my sermons that I have received over my forty-three years of ministry, the one I appreciate most is when someone says, "You were speaking to me! How did you know that I needed to hear this?"

We all want more than anything else to renew the vitality in our preaching. When the new preacher is about to be appointed, the congregation still frequently wants to know if the preacher can preach. Preachers must be able to answer that question with a categorical yes. But can they? It all depends on the criteria we use to evaluate our preaching.

While I may not be able to provide you with a neatly defined set of criteria by which to evaluate your preaching, in the next few pages I will offer guidelines about how to make the invitation during the sermon more effective. I will also outline the basic elements of invitational preaching; this may help you better evaluate the nature of your preaching.

Let us look first at guidelines to keep in mind when extending the invitation near the conclusion of the sermon:

▲ The conclusion should emerge out of the main content of the sermon. Do not superimpose the conclusion on the sermon material.

▲ The conclusion should include an appeal that is consistent with the main thesis of your sermon.

▲ The conclusion is a good place to pull together the loose ends of the sermon by offering a summary of the sermon.

▲ Keep firmly in mind the personal and family needs of the congregation, and speak to those needs.

▲ Use a tone of voice that makes people feel welcome and that communicates loving care.

▲ The conclusion should be brief and to the point.

▲ Use an illustration, quotation, poem, or hymn; or simply ask, "What are you going to do with Jesus?" or "What are you going to do about your situation?"

▲ The conclusion must happen at the proper time. Allow sufficient time for the conclusion; avoid having to rush through the invitation and concluding hymn. I recommend at least eight to ten minutes for the conclusion; this allows you to extend the invitation without rushing people, or ending the service late. The conclusion forms the climax of the service—it merits attention and time. Build in the conclusion as a vital part of the total time of the worship service. The conclusion should also include an appeal for people to accept Christ as their personal Savior and Lord. Extend a call to discipleship, as well as an invitation for people to unite with the congregation.

Of course, my emphasis in this chapter upon invitational preaching does not negate in any way the importance of follow-up and nurture.

Wesley used nurture very effectively with his converts: He made sure that everyone of them attended class meetings. For early Methodism, the class meetings were just as essential as the experience of conversion. Christian education and the evangelistic task must be closely related. Evangelism and nurture must go hand in hand.

We have often made the mistake of thinking that getting a person converted was all that was needed. We made no provision for the new convert to be assimilated into the life of the church; we provided no follow-up, no nurture. It is no wonder that many people fell by the wayside. Personal conversion must be followed by letters, telephone calls, and personal visits to ensure that the new convert is truly assimilated into the life of the church.

The possibility that people will respond to our invitation is always there, especially when the sermon is geared to the needs of people. However, helping people to respond is the work of the Holy Spirit. We do not plan the response, nor do we determine the way it will work; and we certainly don't manipulate people to respond. A sense of integrity demands that we simply open the door and say, "Come in if you would like. You're welcome here. This is your home." The goal of the gospel's power is always that people may be changed; and this goal transcends all others.

The invitational sermon is motivated by a spiritual passion burning within the preacher. It is the same passion that enabled Paul to say, "Woe to me if I do not proclaim the gospel!" (1 Corinthians 9:16). The invitational sermon, therefore, is not a burden or an obligation. Nor is it a job; rather, it is the power of God manifested through preaching.

The invitational sermon leads people to total transformation. It addresses people in the midst of their burdens and personal crises and aims to release those in bondage and despair and to bring hope. The invitational sermon speaks to those who are disenchanted with life, feeling that life has become unbearable. When the gospel is proclaimed with conviction and eloquence, it is like the sound of a trumpet calling men and women to new life.

Charismatic preaching is a term of fairly recent origin. Among the general populace the word *charismatic* is used to describe an extroverted personality that possesses a special charm, a natural knack for engaging others and holding their attention. Genuine charisma, however, is a spiritual quality infused in the preacher by the Holy Spirit. It is sometimes called the anointing of the Holy Spirit. Many famous preachers who possessed charisma regarded it as a gift, a special grace of God. But they prepared by prayer and meditation for the reception of that gift. Followers of John Wesley attributed his success in the midst of difficult circumstances to the prayer chair in his house on City Road in London. In that chair, he would read the Bible and pray daily at five o'clock in the morning. When circuit-riding Methodist preachers in America arrived at their destination, they would go out behind the church to pray for the anointing of the Holy Spirit. E. Stanley Jones, with whom I had the privilege of traveling overseas, religiously observed the practice of spending time alone before preaching a sermon, which on occasion was three times a day. He called this time "the quiet hour," for it was a time for listening to what the Spirit had to say.

Authentic charismatic preaching, anointed preaching, and invitational preaching are synonymous—in all three forms of preaching, preachers trust the Holy Spirit to ignite their souls so that their message is vivified. Charles Reynolds Brown said that all the homiletical techniques are of no avail unless the Holy Spirit empowers the preacher.[23] The special quality of invitational preaching is its focus on the invitation and its reliance on the Holy Spirit to lead the listener to respond to the invitation.

I am aware that many people will ask, "What percentage of those who come forward continue in the faith?" I am also aware of the statistics that show that only a small percentage of those who have responded to evangelistic crusades actually belong to churches and are active in local churches. This is a difficult problem indeed, and nobody has found a simple solution to the matter of a follow-up system to use after people have responded to the invitation to follow Christ.

I am persuaded that many people sit in the pews on Sunday morning with all kinds of personal needs (spiritual, emotional, psychological), whether they recognize them or not. What is missing? There is no simple answer. However, it is safe to say that most of these people are looking for meaning beyond the secular activities, which do not satisfy their inner lives. If this is so, the pulpit presents an unusual opportunity

23 Discussed in *The Art of Preaching*, by Charles Reynolds Brown (The MacMillan Company, 1948); page 248.

to address their needs and invite them to find meaning in Jesus Christ when Christ is accepted as Savior and Lord.

As another way to assess whether a form of preaching is genuinely invitational, let me provide a brief description of some of the essential elements of invitational preaching:

▲ Invitational preaching is based on a theology of acceptance; therefore, it is nonjudgmental and opens the door to anyone who will respond to Christ.

▲ Invitational preaching addresses the whole person.

▲ Invitational preaching acknowledges that human beings are sinful—including the preacher.

▲ Invitational preaching is highly sensitive to human needs and sees people not as what they are but as what they may become.

▲ Invitational preaching deals with real people in the real world of the soon-to-be twenty-first century.

▲ Invitational preaching is biblical, both in content and in basic theological assumptions.

▲ Invitational preaching is Christ-centered, acknowledging Christ as Savior and Lord of both the individual and the society.

▲ Invitational preaching calls people to respond in repentance and faith, but never in a manipulative way.

▲ Invitational preaching calls for a decision about the subject matter of the sermon.

▲ Invitational preaching takes seriously all the emotional baggage that people carry with them constantly.

▲ Invitational preaching leads a person to total commitment, to discipleship, and to the community of faith.

▲ Invitational preaching begins where people are. It acknowledges the reality of sinfulness. It recognizes the flaws and failures of people in our complex society. It conveys compassion for those who are hurt, for those who are disenfranchised, for those who live in constant ambiguity, for those who refuse to live in the real world of the twenty-first century.[24]

I'm not saying that calling people to be converted is the end of the matter—even though conversion is a basic evangelistic concern we all have. Rather, I'm talking about an all-inclusive concept of invitation

24 Discussed in *How to Reach Secular People*, by George G. Hunter III (Abingdon Press, 1992).

that addresses people in all sorts of conditions. The invitational sermon is designed to deal with all kinds of human needs, addressing
those needs and inviting people to respond to something that is challenging, something that includes risk but is nevertheless fulfilling.

Wesley's preaching stressed repentance and forgiveness. He
addressed these themes in most of his sermons. He knew of the despair
and guilt in which people found themselves and offered them the grace
of God's acceptance. His major theme was always justification by faith,
which leads to "holiness of heart and life." Perhaps in our postmodern
era, the time has come to quit inviting people to come to church and
instead invite people to come to Christ.[25]

However, the need to invite is still there! The question is, Can we
find a new approach—and perhaps a new language—to fill that need
when it presents itself in congregations during Sunday worship? I
believe it is possible to rediscover the age-old wisdom of preaching in a
way that addresses people's needs and elicits their response.

In this chapter, I have been calling this kind of preaching "invitational preaching." To be sure, there are other ways to identify this form
of preaching. For example, it could be called redemptive preaching.
There is a sense in which all preaching is redemptive, or ought to be.
Invitational preaching could also be called evangelistic preaching. The
phrase *evangelistic preaching* has been closely identified with revivals
and preaching missions, but I have in mind a more inclusive scope.

Invitational preaching can also be identified as "preaching for a
response"—hence, the subtitle of this chapter. This phrase refers to
preaching that anticipates and expects some kind of response.

To summarize, invitational preaching is the kind of proclamation of
the gospel that not only addresses human needs and people where they
really are but also provides a climate of invitation, both in the content
of the preaching and in the style of delivery.

The sermon of invitation does not call for a return to the fiery styles
of some of the evangelists of a bygone era; rather, it has to do with the
possibility of rediscovering the sense of urgency that is an inherent part
of the gospel. If the message is meaningful to the preacher, and if it
addresses his or her own needs, the element of urgency emerges naturally. Preachers need to be honest about how God has touched their

25 Discussed in *FaithQuakes*, by Leonard Sweet (Abingdon Press, 1994); page 28.

own lives. Fred Craddock uses the phrase "reexperiencing the message" to emphasize this need.[26] Some sermons, he says, are delivered without passion, as if nothing were at stake. Craddock writes: "People cannot live by ideas alone; the whole being has to register the value of those ideas. We call this passion."[27] It has been said that the unpardonable sin for preachers is to be boring. The preaching of the gospel must enable people to "get up and walk" and begin to live. This is indeed exciting!

However, in the final analysis, we know that the effectiveness of a sermon is not measured in terms of its subtlety of thought or ideas, nor in the rhetorical techniques of the rendition, nor in the grammatical perfection or literary beauty of the style (prized though these may be). What is at stake, rather, is a spiritual connection between the preacher and the congregation. The bottom line is the extent to which listeners come alive as a result of the sermon. To what extent do they begin to experience abundant life? To what extent are they touched by the power of the Holy Spirit? To what extent are they motivated to respond positively in the direction of a changed and transformed life? To what extent do they become doers of the Word as well as hearers of the Word?

Successful invitational preaching is a complex matter; a whole constellation of subtle factors enters into it. Therefore, I would like to say a word about the demeanor of the preacher and about the content and delivery of the sermon when the preacher steps into the pulpit and faces the congregation.

In invitational preaching, we cannot ignore the importance of the demeanor of the person who does the preaching. If the preacher experiences the "anointing of the Holy Spirit" an hour before facing the congregation, joy will radiate from his or her countenance. This does not mean that the preacher is unacquainted with grief, has never suffered failure, or has never been wounded or brokenhearted. Quite the contrary; it means that he or she has for the time being transcended personal pains, aggravating frustrations, and feelings of inadequacy. I am not talking about an artificial smile superimposed on the face like a mask; nor am I talking about an extroverted personality. God can use an introverted or an extroverted person equally well. Instead, I am

26 From *Preaching*, by Fred B. Craddock; © 1985 Abingdon Press; page 220. Used by permission.
27 From *Preaching*, by Fred B. Craddock; © 1985 Abingdon Press; page 221. Used by permission.

talking about an inner radiance that is a gift of the Spirit. This is some-thing we cannot manufacture; we can only be an open channel for that grace to flow through us.

We must constantly guard against the risk of conveying the good news in a way that comes across as bad news. This is true not only in our preaching but also in our witnessing. We cannot afford the luxury of coming across as domineering and obnoxious. We need to be honest about our own vulnerability. We need to be honest about making claims that are in keeping with reality. We need to be honest as we point to the truth, which is in Christ. We need to engage people in the journey that is a process by which the grace of God is mediated.

The good news is *good* news as long as we are willing, in our preach-ing and in our witnessing, to identify with the estranged and the alienated. Sharing with another, whether from the pulpit or on a one-to-one basis, needs to be done with humility—not to satisfy our own needs but rather the needs of the other person.

Communication theory teaches that whenever we try to impose ideas on another person, he or she inevitably rejects those ideas. People react with hostility when others try to impose their ideas.

Sometimes the most effective sharing of the gospel is done indi-rectly—that is, while talking about something else. It is a kind of serendipity experience by which we first establish good rapport with the other person before we proceed to tell our story of faith.

This indirect method does not mean that we do not speak with authority and conviction—we do. We need to preach with passion, with enthusiasm, and with zeal. Personal witness, too, must reveal a deep and authentic personal experience with Christ in our lives. Per-sonal witness is not done from ulterior motives or a promise of reward. Rather, we tell the good news because it is the news of Christ's total and unconditional acceptance of us: He loves us in spite of who we are.

If the preacher's countenance radiates with joy, with a passion for the gospel, and with a sense of expectation that something is going to happen, such charisma will create a heightened expectation on the part of the congregation. As Craddock says,

> The preacher understands the dynamic of anticipation, and therefore designs sermons which create expectation with their early promise, but which will delay the fulfillment of that

promise until the listener is sufficiently engaged to own the message and take responsibility for what is heard.[28]

The preacher ascends the "throne" (pulpit) believing that someone in the congregation is eager to hear the sermon and will respond to it. The preacher expects and trusts that "so shall my word be that goes out of my mouth; it shall not return to me empty" (Isaiah 55:11). A sense of expectation on the part of the preacher is infectious; it affects the listeners. With this frame of mind, the preacher is able to use creative ways to hold the listener's attention in order "that the hearer may be moved to respond with attitudinal or behavioral change."[29] An old adage says, "Attempt great things for God; expect great things from God." With this kind of approach, the preacher will speak with zeal and conviction—even a sense of authority—that will establish a rapport with the congregation.

However, the preacher should be careful not to allow zeal or passionate convictions to come across in a tone that sounds dogmatic or domineering, as if he or she were trying to impose those convictions on the listeners. For, as we said earlier, trying to impose ideas on another person elicits resistance, if not outright resentment and rejection.

The tone of voice of some preachers can get so loud that it scares people off. A message is not evangelistic just because it is delivered with high volume. Joe Harding, our beloved friend and mentor of many years, tells of a boy who sat with his father in a church service where the preaching was getting pretty loud. The pulpit was an enclosed structure. As the preacher became louder and more frantic, the little boy whispered in a voice that could be heard all over the church, "Daddy, what will we do if he gets out?" This is not what I mean by evangelistic preaching!

ACCEPTANCE: A BASIC ELEMENT OF INVITATIONAL PREACHING

As I said earlier, invitational preaching must take seriously a theology of acceptance. All people, and especially those who have strayed from the gospel—the estranged and the alienated—must be made to feel that they are accepted as they are. One of the things that children fear most is their parents' anger; and when they are punished, they fear that

---

28 From *Preaching*, by Fred B. Craddock; © 1985 Abingdon Press; page 166. Used by permission.
29 From *Preaching*, by Fred B. Craddock; © 1985 Abingdon Press; page 166. Used by permission.

they have lost their parents' love. The story is told of a man who attended an Alcoholics Anonymous meeting after he was constantly criticized and disparaged for his addiction to drinking. At the meeting he heard about the Twelve-Step Program and heard the testimony of people who were overcoming their addiction to alcohol. After the meeting, someone asked the man, "What impressed you most about the meeting?" Without hesitation the man responded, "The word *acceptance*. I kept hearing that word over and over, and for the first time in my life, I understood what it meant to be accepted and feel accepted."

By definition, the thrust of an invitational sermon is to elicit a decision in response to an invitation; and the climax of the service is the extending of the invitation. But how does one extend the invitation meaningfully and effectively? What if there is no response? Does one extend the invitation if the only ones hearing the sermon are long-time church members? In revival meetings and preaching missions, everyone expects an invitation at the conclusion of the service. But should an invitation be part of a high liturgical service on Sunday morning?

Such questions have instilled an indecisiveness among many preachers nowadays. This indecisiveness stems at times from a feeling of awkwardness, or from a sense that the invitation has become a ineffectual routine, or an uncomfortable intimation to which no one will respond. Part of the problem has to do with the fact that the invitation has become platitudinous. In issuing the invitation, preachers tend to use certain words over and over. Such overused religious jargon must be eliminated totally. Reading great literature, especially secular sources, provides one with an infinite source of new and fresh terminology to communicate the eternal truth of God.

The overuse of platitudes is particularly evident in the case of the evangelist or the preacher-evangelist. Words such as *salvation, sanctification, regeneration, reconciliation*, and so forth, were useful for earlier generations. But people today don't really understand these terms; in fact, they often totally misunderstand them. The invitational sermon is designed primarily to generate experience and feeling, and to lead people to a decision. For this to happen, people need to hear the gospel in a new way and in language they can understand.

Using appropriate language is particularly important in designing the invitational sermon. After all, this kind of sermon is geared toward generating or motivating a response. We all know that words and the meaning of words change as time goes by. Some words become totally obsolete. Likewise, theological terms—even significant ones—can lose their meaning. When this happens, we need to either redefine these words or coin new words so that the gospel may be communicated.

We spoke earlier of how important it is that the preacher truly experiences the message he or she delivers from the pulpit. However, it is also important that the preacher thinks about how he or she wants the congregation to experience the sermon. The invitational sermon is an *experiential* sermon; it calls for the total involvement not only of the preacher but also of the listener. One needs to understand that for an invitational sermon to be effective, the congregation must feel in the depths of their hearts the main thesis of the sermon. The possibilities of what congregation members may feel are varied: a conviction of sin, a sense of relief, a penitent heart, an indescribable joy, a feeling of sadness, exhilarating vigor, the power of the Holy Spirit, inner peace.

The heart of the invitational sermon has to do with changing attitudes and behavior. It is tragic when neither the preacher nor the listeners expect anything at all to happen—and often, in such cases, nothing happens. Is it realistic to say that we must *expect* something to happen? Is it realistic to expect that something must happen every time we preach? I think it is! But one must exercise the disciplines of creativity, arduous preparation, vivid imagination, clarity of purpose, and ardent prayer. Problems arise when preachers do not practice these disciplines—when they expect something to happen *automatically*. This is when evangelism gets a bad reputation.

The invitation to commitment that follows the invitational sermon is sometimes referred to as the "altar call," or the call to come to the "mourner's bench." Both of these terms, especially "mourner's bench," convey an element of nostalgia. Churches no longer have a mourner's bench; however, we do have an altar rail. Sometimes that altar rail is used only for partaking of Communion. I submit that we need to rediscover the altar as a powerful symbol of a place where decisions and commitments are sealed by the Holy Spirit. We ought not to apologize for making altar calls; we need to challenge people to come forward. Let's get back to the invitation business; let's rediscover the frequent use of the altar.

When an altar call is made, the appeal needs to be clear. The preacher's tone of voice should be inviting; it should create a climate conducive to an authentic response to the proclamation. The evangelistic content of the sermon determines the kind of appeal that is extended and the kind of decisions that are made by the listener. Sometimes it helps for the preacher to walk closer to the congregation at the time the invitation is given, because such a gesture creates a more intimate setting.

Invitational preaching proceeds on the assumption that God has communicated God's love supremely through Jesus Christ. Jesus Christ is the authentic and decisive word of God incarnate communicated to humankind. The Word of God (Scripture) describes the saving event through the crucifixion and resurrection of our Lord. The biblical story has the power to overcome sin and elicit a response of faith in Christ. The task of biblical interpretation is to retell the story of God in Christ so as to bring about a divine-human encounter. The divine-human encounter, on its part, brings about new life.

There is no way for the preacher to anticipate a specific response on the part of people; nor can the preacher know in advance how the Holy Spirit will move in the hearts of people. The truth is that as the preacher proclaims the good news, there is always another "voice" (the Spirit of God) speaking to the inner ear and leading people into significant decisions.

People come expecting a liberating word, a word of forgiveness and acceptance—a word that will help them refocus their lives, find win-win solutions, learn to forgive others and themselves, and make wise, responsible decisions.

As he or she ascends the pulpit on Sunday morning, every preacher faces the following questions: Can you really create change in your own life? Can you bring about change in the lives of other people? Can you help people write a totally new script for their lives when they've been handed a bad script? How can you enable people to say yes to new life, without using coercion and manipulation?

Every sensitive preacher knows that on a given Sunday there are people in the congregation who are

▲ experiencing broken relationships

▲ finding themselves in a jungle of frustration and problems

▲ experiencing "burnout" in their jobs, or as parents
▲ feeling the unbearable burden of guilt
▲ feeling overloaded with resentments, anxieties, and fears
▲ trying to get along with difficult people

One of the most serious concerns related to invitational preaching has to do with a practice that says: Come to Jesus and everything will be all right. Such a practice presents a fragmented gospel, to say the least, for it conveys the idea that nothing has to be changed. The person is not required to give up or alter anything. It does not refer to obedience, and it is is totally silent about the demands of discipleship.

There is another kind of appeal, one that invites people to accept Jesus Christ as *Lord*. A total commitment to the lordship of Christ has implications for every aspect of one's life. Such a commitment requires the disciple to

▲ be concerned about and work against all kinds of dehumanizing conditions everywhere
▲ care about the oppressed and fight all kinds of oppressions
▲ be sensitive about the plight of women who are disenfranchised
▲ empathize with the untold struggle of ethnic minority people
▲ be politically involved at all levels of our civic life
▲ feed the hungry and house the homeless
▲ employ people who were formerly on the welfare rolls

Being a disciple of Jesus Christ in the twenty-first century requires asking the question: "What does it mean for Jesus to be Lord in the context of the burning issues of our time?" Such a question is not popular; it is much easier to deal with the personal aspect of our decision to accept Christ as "my personal Savior." To crown Jesus as Lord of one's life and of the structures of society requires a total commitment.

At this point, it is well to remind ourselves of the need to stress grace in our sermons. The fact is, where there is gospel there is grace, and where there is grace there is gospel. In other words, we are not called on to pass judgment on people; rather, we are to open our arms and boldly proclaim, through our voice and body language, that the grace of Christ is readily available to every person here and now. The heart of the sermon should resound with the good news that God has accepted all sinners. So, grace must be the dominating theme of every sermon, regardless of what the lectionary reading may be for that day. We proclaim with boldness and conviction that all people are accepted by God, not because of anything they are or do or say, but because of that amazing grace that is always seeking us.

Preaching effectively about grace requires the daily discipline of prayer and continual surrender on the part of the preacher; it also requires knowing the deepest hungers of the human heart. E. Stanley Jones understood all this very well. He saturated his mind with biblical truth, but he also took time to listen to people and their problems. His famous counseling interviews, which I was privileged to interpret, became a constant source of abundant material depicting the human situation as it is in all parts of the world. As a result, he has been recognized as one of the greatest evangelists who ever lived and, in the estimation of countless people, the greatest missionary evangelist since Saint Paul.

I cannot stress enough the importance of a time apart immediately before the sermon is to be preached. It is a sacred time that no one should disturb. This is why I do not normally try to teach a class between the first and the second worship services on Sunday mornings. Regardless of the vigor and vitality of the preacher, anything other than the preaching of the two sermons tends to drain his or her energies and impacts negatively the effectiveness of the sermon. In most cases, people in the congregation come to appreciate how important this time is. Sooner or later we learn the difficult lesson that you can do only so much and no more.

As I said earlier, invitational preaching must include the element of passion, for there is much at stake. It is a matter of life or death! This is the inevitable sense of urgency that must come through in the preacher's voice. I'm not talking about delivering the sermon with excessive emotion. I don't mean that the preacher gets louder and louder to compensate for lack of preparation; nor am I talking about being anti-intellectual. Rather, I'm talking about putting a little "salsa" (picante sauce) into the sermon.

The invitation needs to be extended in the context of what has been proclaimed. When followed properly, the lectionary provides, in a period of three years, all kinds of motivation and inspiration for all kinds of circumstances and all kinds of conditions of men and women.

For instance, response to the sermon could take the form of a hymn of invitation, a baptism, a confirmation, a profession or reaffirmation of faith and/or reception into membership.[30]

The important thing to remember is that every sermon should include the sequence of proclamation and response. In other words, there can be no true proclamation without some type of response, and there is no response unless there is a proclamation (*kerygma*). Sometimes the response could take the form of an affirmation of faith, using one of the several creeds in *The United Methodist Hymnal.*

At times, people may be invited to respond to some specific action having to do with a problem or a need, either in the community of faith or in the secular community. The point to remember is that the worship service has not ended and is not complete unless the preacher has issued a call to discipleship, with the multiple implications that call will have in terms of the totality of life as it is lived in the world.

Sometimes the most effective way to extend the invitation is simply to include a prayer of silence immediately following the sermon. It is an opportunity for people to reflect on their own lives in the context of what they've just heard. Soft music may be played in the background while the pastor says, "The altar is now open for those wishing to come forward and pray as you respond to the today's message" or "As you remain in the pew, I invite you to focus upon specific ways in which the today's message may apply to your own life."

There are a variety of situations in which the call to respond to a specific invitation would be appropriate, such as the following:

▲ Someone is coming off of welfare and is trying to find a job.

▲ Someone is afflicted with alcohol or drug addiction.

▲ Someone is retiring.

▲ Someone has lost a loved one.

▲ Someone is struggling with the decision of pursuing a Christian vocation.

▲ Someone is going into the military or going away to college.

▲ Someone is ostracized because of race, country of origin, culture, speech impediment.

---

30 See the worship resources in the *The United Methodist Hymnal* (The United Methodist Publishing House, 1989); especially pages 2–5, 736–862.

The whole gamut of the human condition could become the basis for a call to commitment to minister to the specific needs of the members of the body of Christ and the needs of visitors.

At times, the invitation may challenge people to take a special Christian social action in the world, such as involving themselves in the following:

▲ providing services to older adults in the community
▲ helping at teenage centers for social activity and recreation
▲ working to end unfair treatment of immigrants (legal or illegal)
▲ facilitating the process for people who wish to become citizens of the United States of America
▲ providing adequate supplies for preschool and daycare centers
▲ teaching literacy classes
▲ teaching English as a Second Language classes
▲ providing job training for people coming off of welfare
▲ helping support groups such as Alcoholics Anonymous, Overeaters Anonymous, victims and families of Alzheimer's disease, and so forth
▲ working with school dropouts
▲ caring for latchkey children

The sky's the limit! All one has to do is look around a given community (an area where the church is located), ask a lot of questions, and discover multiple needs that are not being met. But it all begins with the proclamation of the gospel and inviting people to respond to that proclamation. It all begins at the point of hearing the Word, then asking people to consider the specific and practical implications of the sermon for their lives.

To summarize, the notion that a sermon has to be invitational and therefore call for a response is inextricably bound to the very nature of the gospel itself as invitation. The sermon must elicit some kind of response to the proclamation.

Whatever else may be said about evangelism and the multiple innovative strategies that abound, I am convinced that the pulpit can be the most powerful vehicle for evangelism in the twenty-first century. Let the trumpet sound and let the clear echo resound around the world, for Jesus said: "Let anyone who is thirsty come to me, and let the one who believes in me drink" (John 7:37-38).

Questions for Reflection

1. What is your definition of *preaching*?
2. Is the preaching you hear today (including your own, if you're a pastor) saturated with passion, emotion, and a sense of urgency? Or is it dull and boring? If it's dull and boring, how could the preaching be changed?
3. What factors hinder you from witnessing to others? What can you do to address these factors?
4. What role do the seminaries play in facilitating training opportunities for clergy and laypeople in the area of public proclamation and personal witnessing?
5. If you are a pastor, would you enroll in a continuing education course? If you are a layperson, would you enroll in a course to help you articulate the faith more effectively?
6. Communicating the gospel today must include learning cross-cultural communication skills, including learning to speak languages other than English. What are the implications of this for you and for your local church?
7. Evangelism and mission cannot be separated. How do we extend the invitation to believe in Christ to the whole world today?
8. Increasingly, we encounter people of other faith traditions, non-Christian ideologies, and new religions. What skills and information do you need to carry on a significant dialogue with them? How would you witness to the supremacy of God's revelation in Jesus Christ to these people?

Chapter Three

Invitation to Healing and Wholeness:

The Unanswered Question of Suffering and Pain

OUR NEED FOR HEALING

W hen talking about healing, the terminology can be misleading and confusing. Sometimes *healing* refers to "faith healing" or "divine healing"; at other times the word means "spiritual or emotional healing." I have heard people talk about the healing of memories and prayer healing. Sometimes a variety of these meanings are used interchangeably. In this chapter, I use the phrase "invitation to healing and wholeness" to include all of the meanings of the word *healing* that were just mentioned.

Invitation to healing and wholeness is the divine art of opening the door for people to be healed—not just physically but for the total personality and from all kinds of brokenness.

Woundedness and blessing go together, as we see in the story of Jacob (Genesis 32:26). Being wounded and being blessed is the true history of our lives and the mystery of our sickness. Henri Nouwen introduced us to the concept of the "wounded healer," helping us see that sometimes it is only *because* we have been wounded that we have the capacity to heal others.[31]

The Eucharist contains two dramatic moments: One is when the bread is broken, symbolizing the body of Christ broken for us; the other is when the wine is poured, symbolizing the healing grace of Christ through Christ's blood. It is at that moment in the liturgy that we gain a new insight into our own brokenness and wholeness.

Many of us have experienced sorrow sometime or another. Many of us have been victimized or abused in some way. It is difficult to erase from our minds the "rooted sorrow." Often, the memory of these troublesome experiences continues to bother us throughout our lives. There are so many people who have difficulty sleeping well at night. Many things can keep people awake at night: being uncomfortable from eating too much, being hungry, being worried, being afraid, being too hot or cold. On the other hand, there are many home remedies for insomnia such as reading a boring book, watching TV, or drinking warm milk or hot tea.

But the real secret of going to sleep at night is to be willing to let go, to surrender—"to die" to all that happened on that day and to release everything into the hands of God, who does not sleep or slumber. Only such surrender brings one to a point of finding total rest.

We all know of miracle healings. There are cases where a person who has been prayed for experiences a miraculous healing. We all have heard of amazing, transforming experiences and how doctors have acknowledged that a miracle has taken place and have finally said, "This cannot be explained by medical science." While one needs to be open to the possibility of miraculous healing, the process of healing and wholeness is usually a gradual process extending over time.

The Westminster Cathedral has a stained glass window made of thousands of broken fragments. The window had been shattered, but now the light shining through the tiny pieces of broken glass is marvelous to see. The window symbolizes the invitation: Is your heart broken? Is your body broken? Are your hopes broken? Bring all the brokenness to the altar and let the great Physician mend it together again.

One of the things that people would like to know about preachers is whether they have ever experienced a broken heart, whether they

31 Discussed in *The Wounded Healer: Ministry in Contemporary Society*, by Henri J. M. Nouwen (Doubleday, 1972).

have ever suffered, or whether they know what it means to be in love. Let's keep in mind that Jesus—the One whom preachers seek to emulate—died of a broken heart. He died of a broken heart and thus is able to heal the broken hearts.

When we are truly honest with ourselves and have the courage to tell the truth (at least to ourselves), we would have to admit that there is some kind of a flaw in our lives. It is precisely the complexity of our fragmented lives, the mixture of good and evil, that baffles us. It is the ambiguities of human existence and the incongruities of life that do not make sense. In the midst of these realities, we read the words of the psalmist: "I have passed out of mind like one who is dead; I have become like a broken vessel" (Psalm 31:12).

I remember well the lady who came to a spiritual retreat carrying a broken mirror in her purse. Every morning she would take out the mirror so she could "fix herself up." As she looked into the broken mirror, she realized over and over again the brokenness of her own life, not just the reflection of her face in the mirror. She shared with other retreat participants: "My life is broken in so many places, my broken mirror reflects only a fraction of my fragmented life. I have come to this place to be glued together again."

In the final analysis, we have to acknowledge that we are all broken in one way or another. We are sick or weak or imperfect or have some kind of flaw in our personalities. But it is precisely in the broken places of our lives that the grace of God becomes real and enables us to transcend our weaknesses.

Our story is a story of brokenness. I can still hear the eloquent voice of E. Stanley Jones reminding us that everything is broken—our dreams, our hearts, our hopes, our promises, our relationships. So we approach Christ, wanting to know if he can put the broken pieces of our lives together again. It is precisely in the brokenness of our lives and when we are humble enough to acknowledge the brokenness that we come to the One who alone can make us whole.

THE GOOD NEWS OF HEALING

Evangelism means proclaiming the good news of the grace of God made known to us in and through Jesus Christ. Preaching is proclamation, but it is not the only way in which we bear witness or spread the good news. Jesus' ministry was not limited to preaching and teaching, for he was also a healer.

As the biblical scholar Alan Richardson has pointed out,

> The formula "Your faith has saved you" is applied to the sick who have been healed (Mark 5:34; 10:52; Luke 17:19), and we are thus reminded that the Greek word [*sozein*] means "to save" and also "to heal or make whole"—a double meaning essential to the purpose of the miracle stories of healing, but one which is not easy to express in an English translation... To heal implies the power to forgive sins (both senses of [*sozein*]).[32]

I have long been convinced that the salvation brought by Jesus Christ involves all aspects of human life, not just the "soul." By the same token, the health of the human body is not something independent of the human mind and spirit. Indeed, this was among the teachings of my mentor of many years, E. Stanley Jones. In India he found total healing, and there is now a plaque on the altar rail of a church in India, commemorating that healing experience. It reads: "Here E. Stanley Jones knelt, a totally broken man, and stood up a totally healed man." As a result of my experience, I now understand more deeply what his teaching (based on his experience) had led me to believe.

The story is told of a little boy who asked his grandmother, who was sewing patches on a torn garment, "Grandmother, what does God do all day long?" His grandmother replied, "God spends all his time fixing things that are broken."

To think of evangelism as an invitation must indeed include an appeal to those who are sick, for the Son of Man came not for those who were well but for those who were sick (Luke 5:31). The invitation is extended for people to find a cohesive center for their lives—to be connected to the Source of healing and wholeness—so that their personalities may be truly integrated, as opposed to being fragmented.

Every pastor and layperson who has made hospital visits knows well that people who are ill are facing an awful crisis. The hospital is an insecure environment; furthermore, it is a strange place, so most hospitalized people experience loneliness, anxiety, and fear. But patients would seldom admit these feelings openly. One has to look for nonver-

---

32 From *The Interpreter's Dictionary of the Bible*, Volume 4; © 1962 Abingdon Press; page 178. Used by permission.

bal communication or body language. Sometimes sick people talk as if their faith is strong enough; yet, we know that when the body is traumatized, faith sometimes is weakened. The patient feels like breaking down and crying, but he or she is not given an opportunity to do so. When could the patient cry? There is no privacy whatsoever and usually there are sleepless, endless nights caused by anxiety and pain.

This chapter encourages the church to be engaged in ministries that take seriously the interaction between minds and bodies. We learned that the spirit can either poison or heal the body. The field of psychosomatic medicine is not entirely new. It has been with us for sometime now, but abundant research has provided ample evidence that whatever affects the mind and the emotions can cause illness in the physical part of our being.

To write about spiritual healing does not negate in any way the crucial importance of medical science, doctors, nurses, hospitals, and the amazing help that comes from professional psychotherapeutic procedures. Rather, it is an attempt to implement what science can do and, in most cases, to walk hand in hand with medical science. If we understand that we are to be stewards of the mysteries of God and channels of his grace, we cannot evade our singular responsibility as clergy and laypeople to bring about healing and wholeness by the grace of the Holy Spirit.

I am not talking about the kind of irresponsible and shallow healing appeal that we often hear through the electronic church. Undoubtedly, these programs help some people, but they also create certain images about "spiritual healing" that are not authentic and that lack integrity. The healing that I am writing about applies to all kinds of circumstances. We take seriously the whole person and not just the body or the spirit separately.

We need to be aware of those situations where healing does not take place. We should have a sound theological grounding that enables us to accept the fact that not everyone is going to be physically healed but that everyone can be spiritually made whole.

Jesus did not heal everybody's bodies, but he made all people whole! In other words, we may not be physically well, but we can all be whole spiritually. The outward healing sometimes is the result of the inward healing. However, if the outward healing does not take place, we're certain that the inner healing is always a possibility. In the ultimate analysis we must affirm that the cross is God's remedy for the human condition.

In Matthew 10:8, Jesus commanded the disciples to heal the sick and to cast out demons. This command is an integral part of our commission as preachers and laypeople, and it is of great importance in our time—perhaps more than ever before. In the light of our contemporary situation, we need to lift high the banner of a Christ who came to heal the sick. Those who are well do not need a physician, but those who are sick do (Luke 5:31). This is true of individuals as well as congregations. We cannot understand what this means unless we are willing to face the reality of our own personal condition. Who can deny the reality of evil in our midst? All we can do is ask, "Is there a balm in Gilead?" The answer is: Yes, there is a balm in Gilead, bringing wholeness to the wounded and healing to the sin-burdened soul.[33] The first step in calling people to be healed is to make them aware of their sickness.

The invitational approach to healing and wholeness proclaims the healing grace of God. This grace is mediated through many channels and remedies, but especially through forgiveness and reconciliation that brings about wholeness to fragmented lives.

The glory of God is manifested as a result of earnest prayer, but sometimes people worry that they don't know the proper language for prayer. Sometimes the best approach is simply silence, for silence is the divine language. We read in the Psalm 46:10: "Be still, and know that I am God!" And after prolonged periods of silence, we come to the point of "letting go and letting God."

I had the opportunity of listening to the famous novelist Kurt Vonnegut give a lecture at Ohio Wesleyan University. At the conclusion of his interesting speech, instead of allowing the students to ask questions, he asked the students a question such as this: "Has there been a teacher now or in the past who has influenced you the most by making you feel important, by making you feel that you matter, and whose impact on your life has made you come alive? If there has been such a teacher, will you please raise your hands?" Almost without exception the nearly 2,500 students and faculty raised their hands.

33 See "There Is a Balm in Gilead," *The United Methodist Hymnal* (The United Methodist Publishing House, 1989); No. 375.

Vonnegut's question proves the point that the people who truly care are the ones who make you feel important. They are not people who are always trying to give you advice or solve your problems. Rather, they are the people who stick by you through all kinds of circumstances. Sometimes these people do not even say a word. They don't need to; the fact that they are there speaks more eloquently than a thousand words. In the silence, they perform a ministry—a ministry of presence and healing.

A PERSONAL TESTIMONY

In the spring of 1997, I experienced a totally unexpected heart attack. This event brought me face to face with my own mortality. I underwent double bypass surgery; and before and after the surgery, I felt sure that I was going to die. I remember well getting up in the middle of the night, right after I went home, to write my own obituary and the order of worship for my funeral. Everything but the epitaph! (It was not funny then, but it is now.)

During the long and slow recovery, I kept asking myself how I would live if this were to be my last year of life. I had many powerful and clear insights, but what sustained me through the experience were the prayers prayed and reassurances received from people across the country. Healing came gradually. I started out taking just a few steps, and eventually walked three to four miles. At first I had to preach sitting down; but eventually I was able to stand, just as I had before the surgery.

One of the insights that came to me during the thirty-day period of recovery was that I would do all I could to proclaim—through preaching, teaching, and writing—the marvelous healing grace of God. It was healing grace that sustained me through the sleepless nights of pain and discomfort, and it was the healing touch of Christ that enabled me to walk again and especially to preach again.

Another question that became more pertinent to me than ever before was, Why is it that some people are healed, and others are not? Human experience has made it clear that it is not because some pray and some don't, nor because some are prayed for and others are not, nor even because some are righteous and some are not. The faithful know it is not because God is careless or capricious. So I had to grapple anew with the problem of evil, but with new insight and understanding, for through this crisis I had learned the meaning of pain and had come to recognize the power of the uncertainty of the future.

Hippocrates, the "Father of Medicine," taught us all that the important thing is not the disease but the person. However, I thought most of all of our Lord Jesus Christ, who went all over Galilee healing all types of disease (Mark 1:34). I can testify with all honesty and conviction that he still does.

I also learned that my attitude was a crucial determining factor in the healing process. I was forced to ask myself, *Do I truly believe that I will be totally healed? Do I believe that prayers will be answered?* At one point, I called two laypeople to come over and pray for me. They anointed me with oil; and from that time on, my attitude was positive, and healing was greatly accelerated.

On the first Sunday in May 1997, exactly thirty days after surgery, I was back in the pulpit preaching. The text I chose for my sermon was John 11:43, the story of the raising of Lazarus. I really felt as if I had gone from death to life.

After my healing was complete, I realized that I had to let go of the control of my life completely, even as I endeavored to reshape my life radically. Yet, I knew that it was possible only by God's grace. My responsibility was to be an open vessel for God's healing. Forgiveness came and so did healing, along with a more disciplined life.

I came out of the awful and wonderful experience of my sickness convinced that evangelism should definitely include the dimension of healing and wholeness. At the time, I was already working on this lecture on healing. During my recovery I was able to write about healing with greater assurance, and with a certainty that comes from personal experience.

I am totally persuaded that healing is more than a matter of intellect. It is primarily a matter of emotion and of the spirit, because it comes down to a decision about whether one wants to live or not live. To choose to live means taking charge of one's life, realizing how much one has to live for.

THE HOLISTIC SCOPE OF HEALING

In most congregations there are people who neglect their bodies. Many of them are victims of the Greek dualism that separates the body and the soul. The Christian faith has a different message: It confirms the unity of body and soul. For Christians, the body is good; it is "a temple of the Holy Spirit" (1 Corinthians 6:19). A holistic message, geared not only toward "saving souls" but also toward healing for the body, can make a significant difference in invitational preaching focusing on healing and wholeness.

The gospel offers a message of healing that includes the total person, not just the soul. The gospel teaches that adversity must be recognized and accepted in order for grace to help us overcome it. The gospel also teaches the importance of loving ourselves, not in a selfish way that disregards the needs of others but with healthy self-love.

The question is, Can the church today rediscover that kind of legacy? Can the pulpit "proclaim release to the captives" and freedom for those who are oppressed? (Luke 4:18). Can the fellowship of the church be such as to include healthy, positive, and creative relationships? Can the church find ways to help people cope with their stress?

Much has been written about the subject of stress as one of the main causes of emotional and physical problems in our contemporary world. There is no question that stress management seminars can help greatly. There are also many relaxation techniques that have been proven to help.

But what about the church, and the teachings of the Christian faith? What about the preaching of the gospel in a way that helps people cope successfully with stress? The gospel has much to say about priorities, making the kingdom of God the highest priority in our lives. The gospel teaches us how to interpret what happens to us and how important it is to respond well to what happens to us. Because of its message, the gospel can help redirect the focus of our lives so that our lives may be productive. Of course, this does not mean that Christians should not build bridges between the Christian faith and medical science—they should.

Negative emotions and attitudes can be obstacles to healing and wholeness. To become whole, we must decide to let go of these feelings. In other words, healing means that we decide to get on with our lives, not bound by our weaknesses or imperfections, but focusing our attention around our strengths.

In concentrating on the scope of healing and wholeness, we must not forget to pray daily for the healing of the whole world. The developing nations need food and resources; the powerful nations need humility and charity. Part of our challenge and privilege as Christians is to bear one another's burdens and to find redemptive ways for the healing of the nations. In one way or another, we need to assume responsibility for the sins and shortcomings of other people and other nations.

The trouble is that most churches have not properly addressed many of the problems mentioned in this section, or have on occasion ignored them. Even church members need to be invited to respond to these kinds of problems in their own lives; the invitation is not just for outsiders or visitors. On an average Sunday morning, there are people sitting in the pews who are totally confused and discouraged, and who do not know what to believe. This is particularly the case when it comes to the relationship between prayer and healing.

THE QUESTION OF WHY

There are people in most congregations who are in denial about their life's condition, especially in cases of terminal diseases. There are others who are angry with God or with themselves and/or with doctors and preachers. Their anger keeps them from being able to cope with life. They keep asking, "Why me?" There needs to be a word from the pulpit that may help people accept their condition with courage and help them do something about it.

But preachers need to appeal to people on the basis of spirituality, not of religion. They need to lead people to an experience of healing and wholeness in such a way that they respond readily. Most people know what it is to experience some kind of existential hell, and they don't want to go back to that condition. Spirituality means moving from such hell to a close relationship with God.

Of course, there are no simple answers to this question of why people suffer—despite the large amount of published material about the problem of unmerited suffering. However, our theological understanding does tell us that God is not in the business of punishing people and sending them some kind of illness. The concept of God testing us is helpful in some situations, but only as long as it leads to growth and a strengthening of character. The main thing, though, is for us to accept

the reality we are experiencing. When we do, we can pray for the
courage to overcome that reality and to be even "more than conquerors through him [Christ] who loved us" (Romans 8:37).

Perhaps the most difficult question with which Christians are confronted is, How can we believe that God's grace is sovereign when
there is so much suffering in this world? Although suffering is not
equally distributed, we know that we will all experience pain, bereave-
ment, and death, and that we will be continually confronted with
human tragedies. This is not a theoretical problem: Suffering is a fact
of life for the Christian and the atheist alike. But Christians proclaim
the good news that grace is sovereign, which means that God is not
limited in either goodness or power, except as God may be self-limited.

Still, we ponder why God permits humans to cause so much suffering for themselves and their neighbors. Moreover, not all human and
animal suffering is caused by human sinfulness. What can faith say
about such suffering? We need to recognize that we usually raise this
question inappropriately. We come before God with our agenda, and
we want to know why God isn't fulfilling our wishes. We don't want to
become ill or unemployed or have our homes destroyed by a flood or
suffer the loss of a loved one, nor do we want these things to happen
to our families and friends—perhaps not to anyone. But is it not true
that we usually question God about such things because they interrupt
our lives, disrupt our plans, our securities, our happiness? In effect, we
are asking God, "Why are you not fulfilling my will?" It is rather
unlikely that we will pray, "Abba, Father, for you all things are possible;
remove this cup from me; yet, not what I want, but what you want"
(Mark 14:36). In other words, the problem of human suffering is
usually based on the implicit assumption that it is God's proper business to make our lives enjoyable. We don't usually pose the question
from the perspective of faith, asking what are *God's* aims for our lives.
When invited to the great feast, we want to determine what will go on
the menu! It follows, then, that the life we commonly wish for is contrary to God's aims; a life that has no real security apart from faith, and
that will continually confront us with challenges to our false securities,
suits God's aims very well.

Jesus' offer of abundant life (John 10:10) is not an offer of carefree,
disease-free, safe, self-indulgence. The abundance that Jesus offers is

the wholeness that comes from reconciliation with God and loving service to our fellow human beings. Hence, while there are many reasons why some people are healed and some are not, we recognize that God's purposes are better fulfilled in a world in which everything is uncertain—everything, that is, except faith's confidence in God's ultimate victory.

So, in the midst of an uncertain and alienated life, God in Christ has invited us to a feast, has offered the security of an inalienable love from which even death cannot separate us, and has given us the joys of serving in love. It is the gift of the abundant life, a life of meaning, hope, and joy, even when we are embattled, misunderstood, and persecuted.

THE CHURCH AND ITS MINISTRY OF HEALING

I'm persuaded that an invitational approach to evangelism must include the themes of healing and wholeness. However, when it comes to the matter of extending the invitation for healing and wholeness, one realizes the importance of reconstructing our image of what this is all about.

In reconstructing the connections among healing, evangelism, and invitation, it helps to keep the following guidelines in mind:

▲ Memory needs healing, especially healing from regret that continues to say, "If only..."

▲ Relationships need healing, especially relationships fractured by estrangement and in need of reconciliation.

▲ Healing means total surrender when a person is able to release all the possible causes of his or her sickness and be free from it.

▲ Healing is the result of patience and the maturing process.

▲ Healing results from the surrender of all negative emotions.

▲ Healing involves daily periods of silent meditation and prayer.

▲ Regular attendance at worship and involvement in the fellowship of a church are important ingredients of the healing process.

▲ Meaningful activity that helps other people aids in our healing.

▲ Healing is helped by daily laughter.

▲ In addition, since healing involves the body also, a healthy diet (including fresh fruit and vegetables, small amounts of beef) and daily exercise are worth remembering.

You may wonder, *What does all this have to do with the spiritual life?* I am persuaded that these guidelines—even the ones dealing with diet and exercise—have everything to do with spiritual health. When it comes to extending the invitation to healing and wholeness, these guidelines, too, are evangelism, good news.

One of the most transforming aspects of the gospel is to believe in the miraculous power of love. There are those who believe that all diseases are ultimately related to a lack of love and that, therefore, all healing in some way or another is related to the capacity to love and to be loved. This is the very heart of the gospel! The love that is most important is God's love. It is grace that makes faith, hope, and love possible for us. We are fragile creatures, subject not only to death but also to profound anxiety due to spiritual emptiness and meaninglessness. But where are we to find meaning, if not from the grace of God?

When someone who is mired in depression, hopelessness, anger, pessimism, guilt, and meaninglessness comes to faith, a profound change takes place. He or she experiences the grace of God, which accepts us in spite of the fact that we are unacceptable. He or she comes to know a love from which nothing in all creation can separate us (Romans 8:38-39), a love that overcomes all negative emotional and spiritual states and replaces them with love, hope, and joy.

There are ministries of proclamation, and there are ministries of healing, and there are ministries that bring these two together. For me, they belong together. I do not, however, wish to endorse some of the well-known televangelists' healing shows. Some of these shows indulge in sensational forms of entertainment, calculated to make a great deal of money for the "healer-evangelist." Also, these shows often convey the impression that only its particular healer-evangelist can provide the healing. To be sure, some people have an unusual ability to evoke responses that appear "miraculous," but that is no assurance that God's healing has taken place. Moreover, if the focus is on the healer and his or her profit, and if the appeal is to people's self-centered concerns about their own health, without a desire to become God's agents, it is clear that it is not the healing that God offers.

Yet, there is a place for a healing ministry in our congregations. This requires that we try to correct many understandings of healing that are superstitious or just plain wrong, and to replace these with an approach that is responsible, accountable, and holistic. The healing message must be proclaimed in the context of orderly worship. It must not exclude the roles of medical science, but it must be done with full awareness that sometimes spiritual healing is the only route to a person's wholeness.

Some people do not recognize that they are "sick." So, part of our healing ministry is to help such people to become aware that they are among those whom Jesus came to heal. The invitational approach to healing and wholeness is the proclamation and sharing of the healing grace of God. This grace may be mediated through many channels and remedies, but especially through forgiveness and reconciliation that bring wholeness to fragmented lives.

The point is that churches have an opportunity and a responsibility to help people see the need of taking care of themselves properly, though certainly not out of self-centered motivations. It is part of the call of God to all people to participate in the ministries of grace; and taking care of our bodies is part of what makes ministry possible. Recognizing the relationships between faith and the reduction of stress, realizing that we burn up a lot of energy in anxiety over things that are of little real importance, and getting our priorities straight are things with which the church can help us. Indeed, it is only faith in God that makes possible a life with right priorities.

So there are many things our local churches can do to help people see the interdependence of body, mind, and spirit and mature toward wholeness. Most important, of course, is the church's preaching, teaching, and living witness to the grace of God, which has been made known to us in Jesus Christ; for none of us will find health and wholeness as long as we live in alienation from God. However, today we know that this must not be understood as meaning that the church's concern is only with our souls. Christian evangelism includes ministries of healing—the healing that aims at the wholeness of the people. Such healing ministries help to extend God's invitation to the Great Feast.

SPECIFIC SUGGESTIONS FOR CONDUCTING HEALING EXPERIENCES

So how do we pray for healing and wholeness? There is no formula, but let me venture a few practical suggestions:

▲ Pray for the sick, followed by a period of silence, meditation, and (preferably) fasting.

▲ Select a place that is quiet and without interruptions.

▲ Be sure the place is properly lit and comfortable.

▲ Encourage the person to be totally relaxed (free from deadlines or commitments), and help the sick person to put his or her mind in neutral and to really listen to what God is trying to say.

▲ Read silently or aloud a portion of the Scriptures, particularly from the Psalms.

▲ If you are praying for yourself, be sure that there is harmony and peace in your inner self, but if you are praying for someone else, encourage the person to forgive and reconcile with someone with whom there is enmity or resentment.

▲ Make sure that if there is anyone else in the room with you, there is *total* agreement and consensus. Be one in spirit and purpose (Philippians 2:2).

▲ Use the laying on of hands and the anointing with oil.

▲ The anointing with oil may take place by making the sign of the cross with the index finger on the forehead of the person, but you may also anoint the hands, the feet, or some other part of the body where the person may be hurting and requests it.

▲ Pray *brief* prayers, and pause and listen; then as insights come, pray some more as guided by the Holy Spirit.

▲ When the procedure is over, sit in silence for a while and internalize the experience, and do not hurry up to the next engagement.

▲ Share with each other any new insights that can be helpful, insights that have come to you during the time of silence that may have some practical help to the sick person.

▲ Give the person several Scripture texts or other significant quotations, and encourage that person to memorize them and to repeat them throughout the day.

▲ Encourage the person to tell others about whatever partial or total healing has taken place.

▲ I recommend that this procedure be repeated every two or three days, or at least once a week. Allow for the possibility of a miracle taking place, but if not, certainly a gradual process of recovery.

Scientific records prove over and over again that during a time of meditation and prayer, there is lower blood pressure, slower heart rate, and other signs of new vitality.

Following a time of meditation, one of the most appropriate hymns to either sing or meditate is the following:

> Pass me not, O gentle Savior, hear my humble cry;
> while on others thou art calling, do not pass me by.
> Savior, Savior, hear my humble cry;
> while on others thou art calling, do not pass me by.[34]

The person who is doing the prayer needs to have total empathy with—not sympathy for—the person for whom he or she is praying. There is an anonymous, ancient prayer that reads:

> Let my soul take refuge from the crowding turmoil of worldly thoughts, beneath the shadow of Thy wings, and let my heart, this sea of restless waves, find peace in Thee, O God.

Questions for Reflection

1. Salvation is healing, reunion, bringing together that which was separated. Think of ways in which this concept applies to your own life.
2. Reflect upon the journey of your life. Have you had significant experiences of healing? If so, when?
3. Does your church hold regular healing services? If not, why not?
4. Do you know other people—friends and relatives—who are sick? How would you go about extending to them the invitation to healing and wholeness?
5. Are there unresolved conflicts in your own life? Is there anger or resentment? Do you feel burdened by legitimate or false guilt? If so, what do you plan to do to appropriate Christ's healing resources?

34 From "Pass Me Not, O Gentle Savior," words by Fanny J. Crosby, *The United Methodist Hymnal* (The United Methodist Publishing House, 1989); No. 351.

A Concluding Word

The gospel is invitation; therefore, evangelism is also an invitation extended to whosoever may come. Preaching is also an invitation to respond to the proclaimed Word. The invitation includes not only those who need personal spiritual salvation but also those who need healing and wholeness and those who would be change agents for social justice. Salvation is the healing of personal and collective evil.

This concept of invitation is based on a theology of acceptance that is grounded in both the Old and New Testaments. It is a theology of grace—unconditional grace (Ephesians 2:8). This theological understanding does not exclude the reality of the nature of God, who in addition to being a forgiving God is also a God of judgment and righteousness.

The invitation is more powerfully and directly extended through the verbal proclamation of the gospel. Preaching per se takes place with the aim of securing a response. The response is in keeping with the specific aspect of the gospel message proclaimed.

The invitation may be explicit or implicit—that is, clearly stated or implied—but it must always be present in every sermon. Every sermon needs to be redemptive and inevitably include the note of grace and acceptance. The idea of invitation may or may not include what is traditionally identified as an "altar call." The response may take place in many other ways in word or deed. Preaching that leads people to a divine-human encounter brings about the new life in Christ as a result of the encounter.

The proclamation of the gospel always takes place in the midst of brokenness in body, mind, or spirit. This brokenness is manifested through physical illness, alienation, or estrangement. These are all manifestations of our human frailty and finitude.

Therefore, the invitation to healing and wholeness is extended primarily through preaching. However, it may also be extended through small-group experiences or through one-on-one dialogue.

The invitation is to a total commitment to Jesus Christ as Savior and Lord, which transcends all other human fragmented loyalties. The appeal does not negate under any circumstances the unique role of medical science and psychotherapy in the healing process.

In the final analysis, it is all a miracle of grace. The miracle of new life and wholeness is something to be expected every time the gospel is preached. It is an ongoing process of nurture, growth, and maturity.

I have come to the conclusion that the church today may be truly revitalized by stressing the centrality of the divine-human encounter through invitational evangelism in the totality of its life and work.

To this end, may I invite you to respond to the invitation and come to the feast!

Shalom!